LITTLE BIG BONG

Mike O'Briant

Copyright © 2024 Mike O'Briant

All rights reserved

The characters and events portrayed in this book are/were real. Some names have been changed to protect those people.

No part of this book may be reproduced, or stored in a retrieval system, or transmitted in any form or by any means, electronic, mechanical, photocopying, recording, or otherwise, without express written permission of the publisher.
890
ISBN-10: 9798322543671

Cover design by:Malcom MacKinnon
Library of Congress Control Number: 2018675309
Printed in the United States of America

TABLE OF CONTENTS

Preface

Prologue

Chapter One: First Time High and Transformation

Chapter Two: Paper Chase

Chapter Three: Newton and the Tuscarora

Chapter Four: Jury Trial Legs

Chapter Five: Chilly

Chapter Six: Enbridge: The largest oil spill on the North American Continent

Chapter Seven: Stuxnet and Panama

Chapter Eight: Back In Time to The Innocent

Chapter Nine: Almost Lost It All

Afterword

PREFACE

This work of non-fiction is my recollection of the events that are played out here. To protect identities, some names have been changed.

This book contains topics that may be sensitive to some readers including but not limited to domestic & sexual assault, suicide, drug use & addiction, along with historical events that include bigotry and racism across the world.

If you are struggling with any of these sensitive issues, please reach out to family, friends, and/or professionals for assistance. Your life matters to the world. Help is available - call or text 988 for the Suicide & Crisis Lifeline.

Sincerely,

Mike O'Briant

Cover & Back Jacket Image Credit - Malcolm MacKinnon (Exclusive & Limited Rights)

PROLOGUE

My name is Mike O'Briant, but they call me Grandpa at the cannabis dispensary in Coldwater, Michigan where I work. I'm about 65, thin and bald, but spry and polite. My daughter just died a few months ago. Her death rendered me talkative, a way of dealing with my grief. I was an attorney, and I represented a sadistic serial killer from Michigan. I also represented indigenous in the United States and Panama. Yea, right you're thinking. Why is he there in Coldwater, at a cannabis dispensary working for tips – you're not a big shot and never was.

Listen to my story. I'll show you. I invite you to Google and research the events I am discussing and writing about. Google the Lansing, Michigan serial killer who went by the name Chilly. You see, there I am. Yes, that is me in the pictures and videos sitting next to Chilly in the courtroom. I was much heavier back then before my stroke. It seems unreal to me now, everything that occurred. So horrific are the murders, I had blacked out and forgotten many of the gory details until writing about them. The horrendous details came pouring back to me once I began writing of the horrific murders. I am writing about Chilly's case in the hopes it will bring attention to his kangaroo trial and help get him a retrial so he can be found not guilty by reason of insanity.

After searching Chilly and his murders, research STUXNET so you can really understand its relation to the Enbridge oil spill in Michigan and the BP oil rig explosion in the Gulf of Mexico. Search for the Tuscarora American Indians in New York and the Ngäbe indigenous of Panama. These are the indigenous tribes that I represented as their attorney in mass action chemical exposure cases.

Here I am telling you my stories like it was yesterday. I will captivate you with the extent and scope of these cases and lawsuits where I represented in multi-billion-dollar chemical exposure cases indigenous tribes in New York and Panama - I married a Colombian prostitute I met in Panama while representing indigenous banana plantation workers - I discovered the hidden and secret cause of the Enbridge pipeline spill and the BP rig explosion and oil spill - and my many other legal and personal adventures. You will admit, it is intriguing. Join me and learn more.

My narratives are a mixture of short stories loaded with background of counterculture, spirituality, and drug scenes. I was stigmatized and branded a hard drug user as a teen. Little did anyone expect that I would eventually graduate from college, law school and become an attorney litigating some of the most critical and consequential legal cases of the time.

As a child I was profoundly affected by the assassinations of John and Robert Kennedy in addition to Martin Luther King. It created a distrust of authority and the government. That distrust of authority continues throughout my lifetime and is reflected a great deal herein. I had some good fights, but they were imbalanced losing battles. I usually got my ass kicked. I was a winner but in a loser's bracket.

These accounts come in a two-book series. This first one is about my personal history and about the legal cases that I participated in. The second is about my race to quantum entanglement. Join me and hear the first part of my story. The proof is out there – have a look for yourself.

CHAPTER ONE: FIRST TIME HIGH AND TRANSFORMATION

It was 1972, the year I would be transformed into a rebel, a hippie, and a druggie. A lot was going on that year. The Munich Olympics terrorist attacks occurred earlier that summer. President Nixon was further embroiled in Watergate. Love and peace were being extorted for greed and profit.

It was later that summer when Joe came over while I was mowing the neighbor's yard. Big money was made mowing yards with a one horsepower manual mower. Joe told me Tinker had found some weed. We were summoned to the hole. The hole was one of our many underground forts. We all worked on digging that hole and it took several years to finish. It was in the middle of a large field. It was invisible to the older generation and cops.

I left the mower and hurried to the hole. When Joe and I arrived, Tinker and Jimmy Baker were already there. They were on the floor seated around a home-made plastic bong. Tinker pulled a bag from his pant crotch area. We passed around the bag. We all chipped in three dollars for it. The first I had ever seen and looking at my first bag of weed, I saw seeds, stems and oregano looking flakes at the bottom of a well-used baggie. It was the remnant of a *lid* of Mexican swag weed. That's all that was available for a long time. It was marihuana that originated in Mexico, bricked into kilos, and wrapped in Mexican newspapers. You could smell that Mexican swag weed from a mile away. Everything but the stock and roots of the cannabis plant, without any trimming, was bricked up and sold for one hundred dollars a kilo at the Mexican border. Broken down for retail, the swag weed usually sold for ten dollars an ounce and it must not have been any stronger than five percent.

Back in the hole, we passed around the bag of five percent swag weed, then we got down to smoking some. Tinker went first. He was a year older than me. He was the kid always in trouble. At fourteen, Tinker had already been through the juvenile system a few times. He lived with his grandmother. Tinker put the home-made bong to his mouth. Joe lit a match and put the flame up to the bowl that held the weed. The weed glowed red in the bowl as the match flame ignited the weed. Tinker's face turned red as he tried to hold the smoke in his lungs. Then a cloud of smoke exhaled followed by Tinker's heavy coughing.

After Tinker hit the bong, it was my turn. Something was in the air. You could feel it. I was ready for a life change. I had reservations, however. There was a strong stigma attached to those who got high. They called them freaks and hippies. Texas had one of the harshest drug laws in the country where they severely punished drug users, even kids. Dad warned me I would develop feminine breasts if I smoked marijuana. By smoking weed, I immediately became a criminal and a freak. I drew hard on the bong and then nearly coughed my lungs out. The subsequent high was not as memorable as the change of life it represented. I felt cool and part of something.

Besides feeling cool and part of something, I also felt normal when I was high. I could concentrate and focus. I had a head injury earlier which left me with a savant brain injury. When high, I would sit for marathon sessions for hours to do my homework and doing bongs. It exacerbated my curiosity. Mom noticed my sudden personality change from bouncing around everywhere to a more sedate teenager.

My favorite way to smoke weed was to use a bong. So much so, my nickname became Bong. I had a cowboy belt with a western trophy rodeo belt buckle with BONG lettered on the back of the belt. I treasured getting high and listening to all that era's music in my parents' parked cars in the driveway. I was too young to drive, but they let me sit in their cars and listen to my music. It was all on AM radio. There were no FM rock stations in my area yet. My favorite was Black Sabbath's Sweet *Leaf* and *The Wizard*. Deep Purple with their album *Live from Japan* featuring their classic song *Smoke on the Water*. I listened to *Smoke on the Water* right after getting high the first time. Frank Zappa's out of this world lyrics and guitar play were exceptionally bizarre. Led Zeppelin's *Stairway to Heaven* was a religious hymn to me.

I really liked to get high and listen to music almost as much as I took pleasure in playing pinball and foosball. Joe and I started playing foosball when I was 13. There was only one foosball parlor, and it was Fat Cats in Midland. Fat Cats was across the street from Dellwood mall in a shopping center and about a mile from my house. Besides foosball, we played air hockey and pinball. But my favorite was foosball. A table soccer game. We played at twenty-five cents a game to the house. In went your quarter with a sturdy push in, a quick release, a plop, drop, and down came ten hard plastic balls about the size of a golf ball. At the end of each goal were ten beads on a wire that were pushed horizontally from one side for scoring. After a score, another ball was grabbed.

Fat Cats exposed me to the counterculture world. It was a gathering spot for those selling drugs and discontent. There was no discrimination in the counterculture and drug sales. Anyone who had any contraband to sell was there. Whites, Mexicans, blacks, we all mingled. I could get anything. I could score acid – LSD. I bought my first hit of acid from a freak at Fat Cats in eighth grade. We marketed our drugs and peddled our ideas of displeasure with the establishment, government, and parents. The older generation, cops, parents, and teachers were our enemies.

My first LSD, scored at Fat Cats, was called windowpane acid. It was a very small piece of blotter paper with a dissolved drop of LSD. It was very easy to lose and misplaced because it was so small. It might have been small, but half an hour after letting the blotter paper dissolve under my tongue, my perception of time began to change. It was exciting waiting for the LSD to take effect and then be whisked away to another dimension. It was difficult to relay and describe the high from LSD unless you are *experienced*. The effects were amazing. I saw and felt many things that were beyond language with a deep spiritual awareness. An overall impulse to improve myself physically and spiritually washed over me.

It was a real *far-out* vibe with unknown colors dancing with nameless and evasive smells. Light beams were sweaty, wet, and oozing. Walls and floors bubbled and boiled. When I closed my eyes, a circus of multi-colored photo-negative images danced in a three-dimensional pattern. An overwhelming feeling that there was more to life than what appeared before me. I learned of another existence behind the veil of life. I continued to eat acid probing for greater knowledge.

But most of all, I liked to eat acid, trip and discuss science, philosophy, and the paranormal. Joe, Jimmy Baker, Marshal, and I would have deep spiritual discussions. Our spiritual discussions became profound as our drug use increased. These discussions are revealed in much more detail in my subsequent book, *The Race to Quantum Entanglement*.

During one of my trips for knowledge, I saw the *river of faces*. It became my persistent vision. With eyes closed, I saw an electric neon river come into focus. It was a river of bright colorful lights. The neon lights reflected thousands of shimmering distorted human faces. The reflecting faces effervesced up and down the electrified flowing river. I had read about one of the Rivers of the Dead. The Greeks called it the river Styx with the dead on the other side. It was the boundary between the living and the dead, a boundary between the conscious and the unconscious. The *river of faces* vision must be, I argue, a reoccurring vision throughout human history. It was, I felt, a signpost or marker on the secret path to the *stone* or knowledge.

Another marker or indicator was being shadowed by 13. It was an annoyance, and a little scary at first. Numbers I came into contact with would be 13 or added up to 13 - my address, my phone number, my student ID all added up to 13. The 13 illusion was another marker foretold of many years ago. The lurking 13 was not stamped onto my forehead but existed in a persistent shadowing illusion of thought. 13 was a side effect of the deep spiritual explorations.

Another side effect of acid tripping was tracers. Moving objects would trace looking like the moving object was being dragged slower in time and space. The object's fading reflection followed the path of past movement - as if time was slowing or dragging. I was looking for the meaning of my experiences. With unnatural curiosity, I needed to know more. I dove into quantum physics, philosophy and the paranormal. I dove deeper into the philosopher's stone, how to live *a good life* and how to achieve it. I explored consciousness, life, and death. I traveled through the oldest and deepest thoughts of man. I was sure other drugs could help me explore the universe further. But then LSD and weed opened the door.

Another effect of LSD was photo transporting. Tripping allowed me to join photographs. When I looked into a photo while tripping, I was transported to the location where the photo was taken. I could smell the smells and hear the background noises and sounds going on at the moment the photo was taken. The photo transporting LSD side effects, like the others, did not go away after the trip was over.

I liked to eat acid and go on trips to school. One particular trip stood out from the others when in ninth grade. Jimmy's friends from UT brought back home for the holidays several hits of extracted psilocybin in pill form. I had never taken psilocybin before. The next day, I dissolved the small tab on the back of my tongue on the bus ride to Austin Middle School. I blasted off. It must be like the exhilaration an astronaut experiences blasting off. I began hallucinating in the first hour class. Feeling very excited, like *Iron Butterflies* were in my stomach, I heard the dormouse say, "don't forget to feed your head".

I was blasting off in the second hour class right there in the classroom. I was embarrassed and tried to hide the multicolored lights from shining out of my chest. The lights were dim at first then they became brighter and brighter until they were as bright as the sun and then exploded. I closed my eyes and saw the river of faces flowing. I realized my room number was 4-13 which gave me a surreal feeling. The light pouring out of me glistened over the whole classroom. As the light left my body, it became watery and poured onto the floor mixing into unknown colors.

I barely kept my shit together during the light show in

the second hour class. Algebra was my third hour class, and my psilocybin trip was peaking. Mr. Torvonin taught algebra in classroom 2-13. He was wiry and tall. He was a nervous man with continuing acne. I tried to take notes until I broke my pencil tip. When I looked up, I saw that everyone in the class was frozen dead-still. Mr. Torvonin was frozen too, caught mid-sentence with chalk in his hand, pointing to an equation on the board. The classroom was glowing and pulsating with bright neon colors. I got up to sharpen my pencil and still no one in the classroom was moving. I looked back to where I was sitting and saw my body was still there. I kept going. When I made it to the pencil sharpener I saw it. It was an indescribable entity that was neither a spirit nor a physical - I could not tell. The entity made a sound of pure knowledge. There were no human words I could use to capture what was transmitted to me.

After the information download, I started back to my seat in the classroom. An electrified sparkling wind raged and pushed against me as I struggled back from the pencil sharpener to my seat. When I sat down, the normal tempo of time returned, looking and sounding like video slowly accelerating from stop to a regular and normal pace. It was my first out of body experience and it answered the question of whether I could exist out of my physical body.

My psilocybin trip eventually passed and so did the ninth grade. It was time to start earning and saving money for a car. The summer after ninth grade summer I spent doing security and watching over oil well pulling units at night for Dad's business. Not an actual drilling rig, but acted as repairing machinery. A pulling unit provided maintenance to an established well. Unlike drilling oil rigs that run twenty-four hours a day, pulling units stop working when it gets dark. The crew and engineers leave the pulling unit alone for the night or weekend. The machinery and equipment remain. There had been some thefts in and around some pulling units and their oil field equipment recently. Dad hired me to stay out and watch over the pulling unit and the site overnight.

The base of Dad's engineering operation was from Carlsbad, New Mexico. I stayed there during the summer. Every evening one of the pulling unit crew would take me out to the location where the pulling unit was located. I used an old four-wheel IH truck to sleep in. I was delivered to the site just as the sun was going down. I was not alone. I had company. Dog was a stray that we found. He looked like a mini–German Shepherd.

Dog and I would get in the truck as the sun set, get high, and listen to scary stories on the CBS Radio Mystery Show. It never rained and the stars twinkled so mysteriously every night Dog and spent together out there. With the sun just coming up, Dog and I were taken back to the Stevens Hotel in Carlsbad. Dog and I spent the rest of the day eating, getting high, and hanging out at the pool. I ordered room service and also ate at the buffet for lunch and got a ribeye for dinner. Dogs always got a piece of steak too. I played Pong in the hotel lobby. It was my first video game.

Tenth grade followed that summer and weed, or psychedelics were hard to find. It was my first year of high school. On the first day Joe picked me up. I was not driving yet. The movie *Jaws* was showing, and I wore my Jaws T-shirt. I never kept up with my grades and my parents never complained about them. I must have been doing something special though. I did not know it until I got my high school class assignments the first day, but I advanced to the next grade for science and math classes. Joe was a bit jealous when I showed up in his physics and physiology classes as a sophomore while he was a junior.

I never had any high school classes with Jimmy Baker. Jimmy and I were shadow figures of each other. There was exactly, to the day, a six-month difference in our age. We could not wait for Friday to take off on a road trip. Jimmy and I went on road trips when I got my driver's license at sixteen. We often drove to one of the local lakes and Pop's place. Our favorite destination was Sitting Bull Falls, a state park near Carlsbad, New Mexico. The falls was a mountain oasis with multi-level pools connected by trickling streams that eventually gathered and fell off the cliffs to form the falls. Behind the falls were hidden caves. It was rumored that Sitting Bull hid out in those caves from the blue coats that were hunting for him. It was an enchanted and mystical place. It was off the interstate and the road to Sitting Bull Falls was long and twisting. My eighth track played Ted Nugent's *Great White Buffalo* and *Strangle Hold*. Other eight track road trip music favorites included Pink Floyd,

Led Zeppelin, Little Feet, and Frank Zappa. Sitting Bull Falls was an enchanted place and was the perfect place to get high, talk and think.

The following year Marshall got into a bad auto accident. His house and driveway faced a busy highway in the country. He was pulling out of his at home driveway when a commercial truck smashed the side where he was sitting. I visited him when he was released from the hospital. He was shriveled and translucent. It seemed like yesterday that I was waiting for Marshal in a Boy's Town bar in Mexico. *In-A-Gadda-Da-Vida* by Iron Butterfly was playing while I waited. Even though Marshal was a little person, he was very popular with the whores. The most expensive whores would offer their services for free to him. When I saw him lying there in his hospital bed in his parent's living room, it was unreal. His parents kept him alive for months in their living room. I visited him regularly until he died. That was real, that was a slap of reality.

The year after Marshall's accident was my senior year in high school. The physics department made a special class for me. I was the only one in that special physics class. I was allowed to experiment and explore anything I chose. I was interested in lasers. I started making 3D photos by splitting laser beams. I had a large sandbox where I placed the laser. The sandbox acted like a large shock absorber negating any outside vibrations. In the big sandbox, I split the laser with one split beam going directly to the photographed object. Once exposed, I would develop the film and on the exposed film would appear the object in 3D. It was a hologram, they are common now, but then holograms were pure magic.

After I was done playing with the lasers and holograms, my interests moved to human brainwaves and started experimenting using brain wave biofeedback equipment. My physics teacher had a connection and he borrowed a biofeedback machine from UTPD, a local outpost of the University of Texas. I started running experiments attempting to manipulate brain waves using the borrowed biofeedback equipment. I introduced LSD to the experiments. I was able to perform one experiment on myself. Using LSD of poor quality, I hooked up the electrodes to my forehead. I was able to easily control and manipulate my brain waves far beyond what could be performed normally. More importantly, I achieved brainwaves outside my normal range. I could also incrementally control my brainwaves. Manipulating my brain waves to pair with someone else's brain waves to enter their mind, thoughts, and consciousness was my goal. Attempting to pair one brain wave with another was my next planned experiment.

Before my big brainwave matching experiment, I had a trip to Big Bend planned. I was smuggling kilos of weed from the Mexican border at Big Bend. I had made three smuggling runs before that last one. The big experiment was on my mind as I drove through the park entrance and pulled into Boquillas Canyon. I drove as close to the Rio Grande River as possible and honked my horn. I heard horses' hooves clomping crossing the river. Mexican riders emerged from the river basin. They were on horseback and wore ponchos and sombreros with rifles hanging on their saddles. "How many kilos" yelled the Mexicans. "Thirty-four", I responded. I had the GM version of an El Camino. A GMC Sprint was red with two white stripes running down the middle. It was a two-seater with a pick-up bed in the back. It hid thirty-four kilos of weed in a false back compartment behind the two front seats. I unscrewed and removed the barrier behind the seats. There was not a lot of plastics back then, so the kilos were wrapped in Mexican newspapers. The weed stunk so bad that it radiated out from the El Camino in every direction.

After packing in the kilos, I sped away. It was forty-five miles from Big Bend Park. I had left the park in record time. All was going well. Just like in *The Last Days of May* by Blue Oyster Cult, *"The sky was bright, the traffic lights, now and then a truck and I did not see a cop around all day, what luck!"*

With luck and no cops, I did not directly go back to Midland. Instead, I drove to Abilene for a Ted Nugent concert with all that weed still in the Sprint. I went to a Ted Nugent concert. Abilene was one hundred fifty miles east of Midland on Interstate twenty. Pop's place was off the Interstate about halfway between.

I made a detour to Pop's to harvest some marijuana plants. Pop lived in town by then and no longer resided out at the home place, so would not have to worry about him seeing what I was doing late at night. I had a stash of swag weed seeds that I planted out at Pop's farm and old home place. I sewed the weed seeds in any moist area near the stalls and corral. I usually dug a long ditch and just spread the seed all along. Several months later upon our return, those seeds usually morphed into a huge plant or two.

By that fall, the seeds had transformed into fifteen feet trees full of buds. That season only one plant had made it through the summer, growing tall in the back of the corral and stalls just outside Pop's old farmhouse. She was a monster and stood at least thirteen feet, well above the tallest point of the old corral. I could smell the weed plant when I got out of the Sprint at least two hundred yards away. It was dark at night and as I was working on harvesting the plant, I could hear swarms of mosquitoes approaching. I quickly and hastily loaded up the plant. I put most of the weed in bags and placed what was left into a backpack I had with me.

The weed I just harvested from Pop's looked great. It was a sinsemilla with no seeds. The flowers were mature and sticky with red hairs. I called it *Rotan Red*. It was over three pounds of weed. I stuffed some into paper sacks and more into my backpack. However, I was so tired that I inadvertently left my backpack full of weed right in the middle of the driveway where Pop might see it the next day. After realizing my error, I drove back to Pop's to retrieve the backpack full of Rotan Red. It was almost morning when I got back. Dad was there waiting for me, standing there with his arms crossed in front of his chest. He was usually away and worked during the week. I did not expect that he would be there. I had stashed all those kilos in my room before driving back. The weed smell must have tipped him off. He discovered the kilos of weed and threw them all away. I was kicked out of the house.

After being kicked out, I got an apartment that was close to the high school. I did not go back to school right away and I struggled to make it back. It was too easy to sleep in and skip class. Quaaludes were becoming popular. They added to my mounting problems. I only had Mexican swag and no psychedelics. The holidays rolled around. My apartment threw a holiday party that later fell over to my apartment.

Tom Gillet showed up with his nurse girlfriend after the

party moved to my apartment. Last time I saw Tom he crashed his motorcycle at the bus stop doing wheelies. He brought meth. He asked if anyone wanted to try it. I thought meth might lead to a greater understanding and deeper thoughts – Man, was I wrong! I went for it. I watched his girlfriend pull out a spoon. She poured a crystalline substance. She then added water to the spoon. A small piece of cotton from a cigarette butt was carefully laid into the spoon's mixture. The needle was inserted at an angle into the cotton. The plunger was pulled causing the milky substance to be sucked through the cotton filter and into the syringe. She took my arm and inserted the needle into my vein. She first pulled the plunger until a cloud of blood appeared in the syringe. She then pushed the milky fluid into my vein.

Just as the milky substance entered my bloodstream, there was an overwhelming chemical ether smell and taste. *That Smell* by Lynyrd Skynyrd comes to mind. The chemical smell and taste were not in the air, it was in my blood. An electrifying burst of energy hit me as she withdrew the needle from my arm. I had such a blast of energy that I started doing atomic pushups. My mind raced making it impossible to think deeply. The meth high lasted about twelve hours. Then it was over. Then came the crash with a major depression. I had never felt so low and depressed. I could feel the deep depression scorch and scald with every breath.

I did not expect depression from that shot of meth. I did not get depressed after the first time I shot up. The first time I shot up and used needles was at the veterinarian's office where Joe worked when Marshall was still alive. Joe worked for a veterinarian who regularly ordered Dilaudid and Percocet for his wife. Joe and I experimented with Morphine Sulfate and Ketamine by dropping onto our weed and then smoking both.

One night, Joe, Marshal and I met up at the veterinarian office. Back in the exam room, we sat in a circle in office chairs. Marshal wanted to go first with the morphine sulfate. Joe drew the morphine into a syringe from a small glass bottle. He inserted the needle into Marshall's shoulder. Marshall sat in silence. Joe then injected Percocet into my shoulders. I collapsed to the floor. I was a puddle of water. It took a while before I could get up off the floor. No depression or aftereffects with those experimental pharmaceuticals, but no deep thought booster either.

But Tom's meth depressed me deeply and wounded my spirit and put me in an emotional downward spiral. I never got to finish my brainwave experiments. I was too busy doing meth and coke. I missed too much school and too late to save graduation. I was not going to graduate with the class of '78. I would have to go back next year. My shame was exacerbated by the lingering meth depression. I felt left behind. I cashed some savings bonds Pop gave me. At several hundred dollars per bond a year, I had around three thousand that I immediately blew.

In addition to meth, a new vexation was arising- cocaine. I shot up coke later that summer. It had an immediate euphoric blast with the strange smell of ether. The high was better than meth but quickly ended with a desperate panicky need for more. I was turning into a bad person. I was now having to hustle, scrounge and steal for drug money. I was out of control. Van Halen's *Running with the Devil* was my theme song. No more searching for the meaning of life. No more brainwave experiments. But Eric Clapton's *Cocaine* song rang in my head.

All I wanted was more meth and coke and I did not care how I got the money to get more. I had stolen money from mom and dad, even my sister. Getting more coke and getting more meth was foremost on my mind and all I schemed about – how to get more. I came up with a plan. I went to my dad's office late at night and ripped out a check from his business check book. I was about to write myself a ten thousand dollar check and forge Dad's name on the check when Sonny Brown and his wife appeared. They were on their way home late and saw the office lights on. Sonny was a longtime family friend who worked for Dad and had troubled children of his own. He knew what I was doing but pretended not to. He suggested we leave Dad's office together.

With Mr. Brown's actions came the realization - I had to stop. *Roxanne* by the Police had just broken the music mold and was playing on college rock station KOCV in Odessa. No other radio stations were playing that new wave sound from the Police. I heard

Roxanne replayed many times during my withdrawal. The weed situation improved. It was a godsend for my tortuous withdrawal symptoms that lasted for several months. Years later I attended Mr. Brown's funeral and conveyed my thanks to his wife for their kind intervention.

CHAPTER TWO: PAPER CHASE

I made it through withdrawals with Mary Jane's help and some LSD. Months passed since I had used any coke or meth. I made it out. It was 1979 and filling out my college application while I watched the Fifty First Academy Awards that year hosted by Johnny Carson. *The Deer Hunter* won five awards, including Best Picture. *Heaven Can Wait* was almost as popular that year. It marked the final public appearance of John Wayne who died two months later. Our local AM radio station, KCRS, was blasting out the hits on car AM radios by Kenny Rogers, The Village People, Dire Straits, The Little River Band, Styx, and Van Halen.

I went back to high school the following year and graduated from Midland Robert E. Lee High School with the class of '79. I applied and was accepted to Texas Tech in 1980. I stayed in a dorm my first year. Weed at Tech was better than Mexican swag, but more expensive. An ounce of Mexican swag went for ten bucks. A quarter ounce of sinsemilla went for forty dollars. I could only afford to buy a quarter ounce a week during my years at Texas Tech.

After graduating from Texas Tech in 1985, I applied and was accepted to T.M. Cooley Law School in Lansing, Michigan. It had only been around for ten years. It is now part of Michigan State University. Back then Cooley Law School was known as a last-chance law school. That is because if no other law school would accept you, Cooley would. But Cooley had a sky-high tuition rate and flunked out half the first-year class. I did not think I could ever get into law school. My undergraduate grades were terrible. It was my chance. I went for it and packed up from Midland, Texas and moved to Lansing, Michigan.

Lansing was Michigan's capital and was sometimes called *Little Detroit*. It had all the vices of a large city. Downtown Lansing had strip joints like the Velvet Touch and Omars. Whores strutted their stuff up and down Shiawassee Avenue near downtown.

I moved into an apartment building in downtown Lansing upon arrival. Weed was much better in Michigan. I found a weed connection right away. I met a couple of upper-class students who turned me on to their weed guys. The best referral was a dude named Jack that lived on High Street. I bought my first quarter pound of Jamaican Lamb's Breath from Jack for four hundred dollars. It was strong sativa that originated in Jamaica that tasted great with a strong high. About that time in 1986, pure Afghani weed appeared. I bought some from Jack. It was pure indica and bright neon green with a lot of very fat spotted seeds. Afghani was the first weed I ever bought gram. It went for twenty dollars a gram.

The weed situation was in step with Eddie Murphy's music hit *Party all the Time*. MTV was playing videos from ZZ Top, Madonna, James Brown, Wham! Janet Jackson, INXS, Michael Jackson and the Bangles. The space shuttle Challenger disintegrated seconds after takeoff in 1986. The Marco's are expelled from the Philippines. Microsoft went public with its first IPO. Two-pound ice balls from the sky in Bangladesh kill many. The Chernobyl nuclear disaster occurred later that year.

The decent weed availability helped me study and keep my grades up. I graduated December 1987 ahead of schedule by taking extra classes each semester. I didn't go to high school graduation ceremonies or Texas Tech. Graduating from law school was special. I don't think I've ever been so proud!

After graduation from law school, in order to practice law, I had to take and pass the Michigan Bar exam. I was scheduled to take the Michigan Bar exam that spring of 1988. I took a bar review class every day for eight hours for three weeks. I would not have passed the Bar exam without the review class. Graduating from law school alone did not provide what I needed to pass the Bar exam. Everything needed was hand delivered by the Bar review class.

After preparing and studying for the Bar exam, I was ready. The exam was a two-day, eight hour each day test breaking an hour for lunch. I got high before, during and after testing each day of the testing. On the first day, as I waited to take the Bar exam, I saw several others waiting to take the exam that had graduated well before me. They had taken the test many times and did not pass. I thought for sure that I would not pass the Bar exam either. Yet, I passed the Bar the first time.

Once I passed the Bar, I interviewed with several law firms. I also interviewed with a county prosecutor's office, but I ended up working for $17,500 a year at an insurance defense law firm in Sault Ste. Marie in the UP of Michigan. It was right on the US and Canadian border and known as the snowiest place in Michigan. There was a larger Sault Ste. Marie on the Canadian side.

I moved to the Sault in the summer of 1988. The law firm had an office directly across from the Chippewa County Courthouse. The firm was a conglomerate of retired circuit court judges, and some hotshot UP lawyers. The firm usually represented and defended insurance companies against accident claims, mainly auto accidents. The firm also handled criminal and civil cases as they came in.

One group of their criminal clients came in yearly. There was a whore house in the Sault on the US side. Maw's whore house was in a large mansion located near the river. A madam named Maw ran and owned it. She always paid her state and federal taxes. About every year, Maw's place would get raided and the johns and whores arrested by the local sheriff. The law firm I worked for always represented the girls. I was assigned to represent them that year.

I had never represented anyone or anything, much less representing a bunch of prostitutes. It was my first court appearance. I did not know it, but I was set up by the senior attorneys. The girls' first scheduled appearance was a pre-trial conference. Everyone had a good laugh on me. The ladies appeared in their nightgowns, and they tousled their gowns all over me in court for my embarrassment. Then all the firm's lawyers came out like a surprise party. The presiding judge, all the girls and all the firm's lawyers proceeded to get drunk and party in the courtroom. There were a couple of lawyers that got high, and we went out back and smoked a joint to celebrate my first court appearance.

There was a large turnover of lawyers in Sault Ste. Marie law firm, and I was teasingly asked if my name on the door was in watercolors. I did not last long. Six months later, I was working for another firm in lower Michigan that specialized in accidents. The new law firm took every kind of accident. Of all, I preferred automobile accidents. I got good at reconstructing accidents and calculating associated damages for our client's injuries and medical bills. I really enjoyed reading medical records, especially operative reports from the clients' surgeries. The new firm was established on medical malpractice cases. There was a large photo hanging in the reception room with an X-ray photo negative displaying a pair of hemostats left in one of their client's stomach cavities. I soon had a conflict and was fired for calling the managing partner an asshole.

Just about the time I was fired for the asshole comment, I got a call from Dad. Pop had just died. I made immediate arrangements to go to Roatan, Texas for his funeral. I had not been back to Texas since I left for law school. I flew from Detroit to Dallas and then Midland, Texas. I had a three-hour layover in Dallas. There at Dallas airport, I walked out to the parking lot to smoke a joint. I got about half way through the joint, when out of the corner of my eye, I saw a cop diving towards me. Just as he tackled me, I swallowed the lit joint. He tried to dig it out of my mouth. He frisked and checked me all over. I had nothing but a pack of papers for which he threatened to arrest me. I walked back into the airport and onto my plane to Midland very dischuffed after the encounter. If the cop had checked my baggage on the plane, he would have discovered a treasure trove of weed and hash I was bringing from Lansing. When I arrived in Midland, I did not waste any time getting my baggage full of contraband and getting the hell out of there.

After leaving the airport in my rented car, I drove through Midland. It was different. Midland had gone through a depression caused by slumping oil and gas prices. Many downtown office buildings were shuttered and abandoned. It looked different, more run down from what it was. It looked like a ghost town.

I drove two hours to Rotan after driving around Midland. I arrived and went to the funeral parlor. As I entered the funeral home, two men were talking about Pop. I could hear them talking, approaching them and entering the funeral home. I overheard them say something about Pop's spending time in prison. I almost jumped on them. They were talking about Pop. "What the fuck you talkin' about? What did you say about my grandfather?" I said in a loud voice. Loud enough that Dad came out to see what was going on. He stepped between me and them. I looked at Dad. How he had changed. "Come on Mike. Let's go sit down", he said, pulling me away. "This is not the time or place to get into a fight". I had not seen Dad since he kicked me out years ago.

We entered the viewing room where Pop lay. I looked at Dad, still ready to fight and asked, "What the fuck were they talking about - Pop in prison". He said, "calm down. I never wanted to tell you, but your grandfather killed a man in a bar fight in Abilene years ago. He ended up going to prison in 1921". I had not seen my dad or Pop in a long time and now I was at Pop's funeral. Pop - the person in my life I always loved and respected, now, was not quite as I knew him. I was unsure how to react.

After the ceremony, I drove with Dad to the cemetery. I watched them lower his casket into the ground. I watched flowers blow in the wind. After most everyone had driven away, I walked around and smoked a joint. I got to say bye to Pop. Any innocence I had remained at the cemetery that day.

With innocence gone, I rode back after the burial with Dad. On the way, we drove out to the old home place. He grew up there and was delivered on the kitchen table in 1935. The same place I stayed with Pop many summers. It was almost unrecognizable. The old house had been plowed. There were a few remnants sticking out of the ground pointing with anguish at the sky. The corral, pig pens and the saddle room were still there, but in post-apocalyptic condition. The god damn saddle that I used to ride Midnight to town after the big flood was still there hanging in a stall like a ravaged ghost. There was the place where I cut down the large Rotan Red marijuana plant after my Rio Grande smuggling trip and Ted Nugent concert. The trip that led to me being kicked out of the house. It hurt to see it all again, to see Dad again only to be reminded of my fuck-ups.

I met dad back in Midland. I stayed a few days with him

at his home. It was, at the least, awkward and disheartening. Dad and mom divorced when I was at Texas Tech. Mom took off to Dallas with Dog. Dog got out of her backyard in Dallas and ran off. Soon after their divorce, Dad remarried a woman from Ireland. She had two young children from a recent divorce. They were all living together. It was surreal seeing mom replaced with another woman with unfamiliar children in the background. It was evident, however, that I was still branded from my past drug usage. I was still a disappointment. In their eyes, I never stopped using drugs and would always be a thief, never to be trusted. I was still *no good*. I graduated from Tech, went to law school, and passed the Bar the first time. It did not matter to Dad. He did not even know about my abysmal withdrawal from meth and coke after he kicked me out. Once tainted, always tainted.

CHAPTER THREE: NEWTON AND THE TUSCARORA

After Pop's funeral, I went back to Lansing, Michigan. However tainted, I was still a lawyer. I just started practicing law solo and snatched whatever case or client I could find. I mainly took divorces, rental disputes, and all types of accidents. Seeing someone with an injury in public, I would solicit them. Eventually I saved enough money and did some cheap late-night advertising. I got lucky and acquired a few good auto accidents. After a while, I had some savings and was making a regular income from the caseload.

My law practice was growing, but I still had something to prove. I wanted to return to Texas. After five years of practice in Michigan, I waived into the Texas Bar and moved to Katy, a suburb of Houston. It was at this time I met Newton Schwartz - the godfather of mass and class action lawsuits. A neighbor that had done some contract typing for Newton set up the introduction. She set up the meeting at a breakfast place on a Saturday. Benton Musslewhite, another attorney, was with him. At the meeting, Benton was nicely dressed but the other guy, Newton, was wearing an old brown blazer with worn shoes. He did not look at it and I did not know it at the time, but Newton was a billionaire and he had been practicing law longer than I had been alive. He was the wealthiest attorney in Houston and probably in all of Texas too. Before accumulating his wealth, Newton was in the Navy during WWII and came back after the war and graduated from the University of Texas law school in 1954.

At the breakfast meeting, I kept focusing on Benton, thinking "who was this old dude wearing secondhand clothes?". Newton was quiet and let Benton do the talking. I never realized Newton was the money man until we were leaving. Newton finally spoke to me. He must have felt sorry for me because he asked me to come up to his office to talk about assisting with my meager cases.

I went to Newton's office downtown Houston. It was not an office but a fortress. Secured parking, with a trap door entryway to the stairwell leading up to the offices. The stairs and parking entrances had video cameras everywhere. Buzzer doors and bullet proof windows surrounded the building. The office area was above ground. It contained a whole city of legal offices, conference rooms and a restaurant. There were computers and printers churning out work. The massive copiers were loudly making endless copies.

I was led from the waiting room to Newton's private office. There he sat at his desk with people in line to see him and ask for money - most of them. Secretaries with documents in their hands were vying for his attention. His phone was constantly buzzing and ringing. I looked around his office and saw it was cluttered with accident models from previous cases that he either tried or financially backed. In the clutter was an offshore drilling rig lawsuit exhibit, a helicopter model, and airplane models from past accident trials. They were awkwardly displayed like so many trophies. Stacks of deposition transcripts open with sticky notes all over them were on the floor. Piles and piles of folders were on his desk and surrounding tables too.

Newton saw me through all the obstacles in his office and summoned me up front and center. I presented my two cases. One was an oil field accident resulting in death. The other was a mere low injury auto accident. However, he listened to me patiently. When I was done, he called Linda, his secretary accountant. He asked me how much I needed. I was broken, no money and almost starving at that point. Behind in bills and the mortgage, I panicked and spit out a large number. He had Linda write the check.

I was amazed at his humbleness. Humble does not mean weak. Newton was a powerful man. Federal and state judges honored and feared him. Newton had a remarkable litigation history. Newton represented those who could not protect themselves. He was the lead attorney in the Agent Orange litigation which resulted in settlements for veterans and their families. He was involved and had his hands into most mass and class action cases from 1980 to 2022. He was working on some cases in Corpus Christi, Texas.

After he signed the check, he asked me if I wanted to help him with one of his cases in Corpus Christi. I agreed to help him out. He had an office in a renovated apartment building in Corpus. Newton was supporting an ongoing discrimination and product liability case pursuing damages for Hispanic workers at the Corpus Christi Army Depot. The lawsuit alleged Hispanics, a minority class, were treated differently than their white counterparts. The lawsuit alleged that Hispanics, unlike the white employees, were not given appropriate protection from the cleaning solutions used on army helicopter parts. Many Hispanic depot workers developed cancer from the unprotected exposures. The government had immunity, but the manufacturers of the chemicals did not.

In addition to the army depot, Corpus Christi had many oil refineries. On a regular basis a refinery would explode, release toxic gasses or a storage tank would regularly leak releasing thousands of gallons of crude oil. The neighborhoods surrounding the Corpus refineries were predominantly low-income minorities. Minority-dominated neighborhoods were exposed disproportionately to white neighborhoods in Corpus. Newton explained that it was *environmental racism* - when big businesses intentionally polluted or continually ran a polluting endeavor on or next to minority dominated neighborhoods. The environmental racism cases were always mass action tort cases. In mass action tort cases, each member of a multiple plaintiff litigation is individually represented. In class action cases, one or two named plaintiffs represent all persons in that particular class.

About this time, Joe's dad got hold of me. He could not find Joe. He wanted my help finding him. I had not seen Joe since he left for college, my senior year of high school. I could not find him at first. I called all our old friends. No one had seen or heard from him in years. I searched further and found him. He was incarcerated in a Texas penitentiary. I contacted him. He was in a halfway house in

Houston. Joe had been convicted of home invasion and burglary. He had been sentenced to five years. Joe was at the end of his sentence when I found him. I made arrangements to pick him up for a Sunday visit from the halfway house. I saw him a few times once he was released. He eventually married a woman from the Philippines. The last I heard, Joe had a daughter and was driving a truck cross country and living in a trailer on a piece of land in Midland.

Back in Corpus Christi, one of Newton's clients had a medical malpractice case for a botched skin graft and transplant. I took over the case and filed suit for his malpractice claim. The client had a burn injury to his hand, including his palm. He had a reconstructive skin transplant and grafting performed. The surgeon removed skin from the patient's ass to repair and graft onto the burned hand. The ass-skin graft covered most of his palm. Once the skin graft set in, ass hairs began to sprout in the palm of his burnt hand. It was a hairy hand case.

While working with the hairy hand client, the Koch refinery in his neighborhood released hundreds of gallons of crude oil from a ruptured storage tank. His neighborhood was shut-in-place. I took the initiative and had him sign a retainer contract. The client let me meet with his neighbors at his house. I invited the neighborhood for a sign-my-retainer-contract fried chicken dinner. I had a KFC contract signing field day. By the time it was over, KFC was out of chicken, and I had signed about 700 of those affected in the neighborhood.

About that time, Selena, the remarkable Hispanic singer from Corpus Christi, was breaking into the American music market. I wasn't working out of Corpus Christi when Selena was murdered. However, I had a civil jury trial at the same time at the Harris County Civil Courthouse in Houston, Texas, right across from where Selena's murderer, Yolanda Salvidar, was tried and convicted. Once the guilty verdict was released and announced, all downtown Houston motorists stopped and honked their horns for over ten minutes.

I was going back and forth between Corpus and Houston. When I was in Houston, Newton let me work out of Benton and John O'Quinn's offices. Benton was a trial attorney - one of the best.

Benton was on the One World Now crusade and that drove Newton crazy. Even with all his problems, Newton respected Benton and admired him because he was one of the best trial attorneys in Texas.

Benton shared a two-floor suite in a downtown Houston office building with John O'Quinn. Newton owned the building. O'Quinn was a Texas trial lawyer. Among his biggest case wins was a one billion verdict in 2006 against Wyeth Laboratory for its diet drug, fen-phen. He also had a seventeen billion tobacco settlement, and a one hundred-million-dollar settlement against Dow for the silicone breast implants debacle. Newton got his share out of everything O'Quinn won or settled.

I was with O'Quinn in his office when the 60 Minutes TV program interviewed him about his Dow implant settlement. He had just hit it big with that settlement. Of course, Newton was backing him all the way. With Newton's help, O'Quinn became so wealthy that he had the largest car collection in Houston. Along with wealth came his ideocracies. O'Quinn liked to drive his sports cars naked and high on cocaine. His family disapproved and convinced O'Quinn to hire a driver. One night O'Quinn pushed his driver into the passenger's seat and jumped into the driver's seat.

Before O'Quinn's death, I took new client calls coming into their office. I also took calls Benton did not want to deal with. One such unwanted caller Benton did not want to face was Doug Anderson. Doug was a member of the Tuscarora tribe of the Iroquois Six Nations in New York. The whole group was sometimes called *Haudenosaunee*. O'Quinn sped off driving in Houston, in rainy weather at a high speed, naked and high on cocaine. His sports car struck a curb, crossed a grassy median and flew into three lanes of oncoming traffic and finally crashed into a tree. O'Quinn and his hired driver died at the accident scene.

Doug was a natural *Haudenosaunee* leader. His grandfather, Wallace *Mad Bear* Anderson, was an outspoken Tuscarora leader. He led protests against the illegal taxing of Tuscarora tribe members. Doug's grandfather also fought and led protests against the theft of Tuscarora land stolen for the construction of the reservoir right on their land bordering the Niagara River. Mad Bear organized and participated in attempts to physically block the reservoir's construction. He flattened construction truck tires and organized human roadblocks. The matter eventually made it to the US Supreme Court which ruled against the Tuscarora Nation allowing their land to be purloined.

Just as fired up as Mad Bear, Doug explained over the phone that the Tuscarora Nation was just upriver from Niagara Falls in New York. It was also down river from the Love Canal. He told me in 1980, President Jimmy Carter declared the Love Canal a national health emergency. Chemical companies had dumped thousands of tons of dangerous chemicals and other toxic waste material in and around Love Canal. Just down river from the Love Canal were many chemical dump sites on the Tuscarora Nation. The Tuscarora Nation's lands similarly were used illegally by many local industrial companies as a chemical dump ground. Official records and documents verified that nuclear sludge, remnants of weaponized plutonium, was buried on the Tuscarora Nation. These dump sites, Doug claimed, were the cause of a high number of cancer clusters and birth defects on the Tuscarora Nation.

Trying to draw attention to the cancers and birth defects, Doug begged Benton to come visit the Nation. Benton had a reputation for winning big money in mass action chemical exposure cases, of course, with Newton's financial and reputation backing him up. Benton did not want anything to do with Doug. He refused Doug's calls every time. He warned me to stay away from that case because it was trouble. It sounded like a good case to me, and I could not understand why Benton did not want to pursue Doug's case. Doug asked me to visit the Tuscarora Nation to see if I could come back and persuade Benton to take the case.

I had every intention of convincing Benton. I agreed to visit Doug and the Tuscarora Nation. I flew into Buffalo, and I was waiting outside of the airport in the pickup area when Doug and others arrived. Not what I expected, however. Doug and the others were in an old van with salted-out door panels and dirty smeared windows. A cloud of weed smoke escaped when they opened the van side door.

Through the smoke cloud, Doug appeared from the sliding side door. He had long thin tangly hair. With a barrel chest and at least three hundred pounds. He was around six and a half feet tall. He introduced himself and then the others in the van. Crandy and Randy Johnson were in the smoke-filled van as well. They were brothers and both were respected shamans (preacher-wizards) in peyotism and the Native American Church I would find out later.

From the airport, I was given a tour of the Tuscarora Nation. Part of the Nation bordered the Niagara River within a mile of Niagara Falls on the American side. There was a huge reservoir dug out of the Nation's land. The reservoir was fed by the river for hydroelectricity. It was a great source of revulsion for Tuscarora members. We drove around upturned foul-smelling plots of land near the river. Some of the illegal dumping was done on the riverbank by barges carrying the contaminants. Chemical company trucks trespassed onto the Nation indiscriminately dumping on the ground their toxic trash for over sixty years. Doug took me to the restaurant where his sister worked. There she was with a group of women. They were lined up carrying children. Each child had a gruesome birth defect they wanted me to see.

From that hideous meeting, Doug took me to the hotel. We talked for a while, and we smoked some weed. He had some home grown. It was like the Mexican swag I grew up smoking. His brother, Joe Anderson dropped by. His brother was a famous entrepreneur. He started selling cigarettes from an abandoned trailer on the edge of the Nation. Selling cigarettes from that abandoned trailer blossomed into an empire. *Smokin' Joe's* empire.

The next day Doug took me to see Joe's empire. I toured *Smokin' Joe's* manufacturing facility. It was a sprawling commercial site with storage and cigarette manufacturing buildings. There was also an athletic center for his employees. They were big into kickboxing and La Croix.

Smokin' Joe dressed nothing like his brother, Doug. *Smokin 'Joe* wore expensive suits, shoes, and ties. Doug wore secondhand clothing and worn-out shoes. *Smokin Joe* had a nice car and lived in a huge house off of the Nation. Doug drove an old Chrysler van and lived in a burned-out gas station on the Nation. *Smokin' Joe* looked fresh and crisp. Doug looked worn and tired. But it was Doug that brought attention to the chemical exposures and he tried to get some legal help for the members of his Nation.

When I first started going up to Buffalo New York to try to help, I was still doing work out of Newton's Corpus Christi office. It was the spring of 1997. I was living in a house in Katy, Texas and driving back and forth to Corpus Christi. Katy was just west of Houston on Interstate twenty known as the Katy Freeway. I also had an apartment in Corpus Christi.

While at Corpus Christi, on some weekends, I would go to the Texas-Mexican border. Mostly to Del Rio and Acuña, and sometimes down to the Valley. I went across it many times to Boys' Town. It was a sectioned off part of each town in a five-block square area protected by the government officials and the Federales. Boys' Towns were filled with whore houses and bars, restaurants, and rows of small rooms. In each small room was a whore and her bed. If her door was open, she too was open for business. If the door was closed, she was temporarily on duty and unavailable. Probably twenty to thirty customers a night went through each small room. Trash cans in their small rooms were filled with used condoms. Before the gang wars started, there were Mexican Boys' Towns all along the border except in Brownsville.

In addition to all the Boy's Towns along the Mexican border, there were also self-serve pharmacies everywhere. To fill a prescription, I just walked right in and told them what I wanted. The Mexican pharmacies would fill any orders without a prescription. I wanted to experiment so purchased two sixty-count bottles of valium. Vallum was a benzo with a quick half-life. I did not know at the time, but Valium was very addictive.

On the way home from a border vacation, while bonging, I took one of the blue Valium pills. I thought it might enhance the weed. Nothing happened immediately, so over several hours, I took three more. I did not realize the effects until after several days had passed and I could not remember the last leg of the trip home or a few days after my arrival. I took Valium while traveling everywhere including my many trips to the Tuscarora Nation in New York. It removed any inhibitions. Valium made me wild, aggressive, and mean.

While wild, aggressive, and mean, I stayed for weeks at Doug's burned-out gas station. His place acted as my living and working quarters. I was signing up members of the Tuscarora Nation and working on the case. I was also conducting research on the sources and locations of the multiple chemical dump sites. It was staggering how many chemical companies dumped tons of poisonous and radioactive materials on the Tuscarora Nation.

Doug and his friends tried to help the best they could. They set up meetings, ran errands and helped keep everyone informed. Crandy Johnson and his brother Randy befriended me. I spent a lot of time with them. I learned more about Crandy's and his brother's position as the religious men of the tribe. Not only were they tribal traditional healers, but they also acted as shaman for the entire Iroquois Six Nations. The Iroquois are a combination of individual tribes. The Mohawk tribe, another tribe in the Iroquois Nation, provided policing and warriors. The whole of the Iroquois Nation was their parish and the Nation members were the flock.

During my time on the Tuscarora Nation, I met members of other tribe members of the Iroquois including members of the Mohawk Nation. I was then invited to the Mohawk Nation in Quebec Canada. During my Mohawk Nation visit, I met several tribe members who participated in *Oka*. In 1990, Mohawks erected barriers to prevent continued expansion on their lands after a Canadian court ruled against them. The court ruling allowed for a large expansion for a golf course and sixty condos on Mohawk land. The Mohawk militia kept the Canadian government forces in check causing the Canadian feds to eventually back down from their attempted land grab.

The Mohawk invited me to attend one of their longhouse gatherings for a tribal celebration. I watched as the Mohawk warriors entered the long house in full costume dress from one side while the woman entered from the opposite side of the longhouse. The Mohawk women were beautiful, and they all had straight long black hair with olive colored skin. They were perfect, like dolls.

After visiting their longhouses and watching their ceremonies, they showed me their arms stash. Members of the Mohawk militia took me to their weapons cache. In addition to many small arms, the Mohawk militia also had larger weapons. I saw mortars, hand grenades and ammunition of all kinds.

In addition to the Mohawk visit, I was also invited to participate in a cross-country run to memorialize the Second Wounded Knee. Doug had introduced me to Dennis Banks. He was a direct participant of the Second Wounded Knee which began on February 27, 1973, when approximately two hundred followers of the American Indian Movement seized and occupied the town of Wounded Knee, South Dekota. Banks and those running across America with him were members of American Indian Movement, AIM, and the American Peyotism movement. Peyotism was a native American religion. It was a mixture of Christianity and native American beliefs.

There are several tenants and beliefs, but all members used peyote as sacrament during religious ceremonies. The practice originated in the southern territories, and they regarded peyote, cannabis, and mushrooms as sacred. Peyotism was a widespread indigenous religion among the Native Americans and still is today. First Nation peoples and Mexican indigenous made up most of its members. Peyote allows one to communicate with the Great Spirit. Crandy and Randy were indigenous alchemists and were experts in mixing peyote, cannabis, mushrooms and other sacred herbs, and prayer for a desired effect. They never used it to get high, he said. Peyote, cannabis, and mushrooms were used strictly for ceremonial and medical needs. Tripping was considered spiritual in every tenet of peyotism.

It was the Tuscarora Nations duty to provide medicine and religious guidance to the whole Iroquois Six Nation members. Their primary medicine was cannabis, peyote, and mushrooms. A lot of the Tuscarora members were growing cannabis and practiced some limited alchemy. Cannabis was sacred to them. Cannabis seeds, they believed, were tears from the Great Spirit.

I was lucky enough to attend some traditional ceremonies with Crandy and his brother. The first ceremony I participated in was a *false face* mask ceremony. Through a mixture of peyote, cannabis, and mushrooms, Crandy could prepare a special concoction for healing or magical purposes. He could make a mixture used to heal a stomach ache as easily as he could create a mixture that would transport him far away or to see into the future. He had another recipe that was to look through another person or animal's eyes. The *false face* mask allowed the user to go into the other world incognito and hidden from any evil spirits that might hinder one during the trip.

Crandy handed me a wooden mask. The mask had been carved from a special ceremonial tree over one hundred years ago. It had a small opening for the mouth and eyes. After consuming his magic mixture, I put the mask over my face. I followed his chanting. Crandy asked who I wanted to see. I wanted to see my children who I missed so much and who were so far away in Michigan. I repeated his chants and started smoking his specially concocted mixture. As I exhaled, I was transported to my house in Houston and saw my children sleeping peacefully. I spent a lot of time with Crandy. He was very interested in my visions. I told him about the river of faces and how time had stopped in math class. Crandy told me I was very lucky to have such visions. He was really interested in stalking number 13.

From Crandy, I learned to mix different alkaloids and herbs. I was becoming an alchemist. I learned many of the chants and songs of peyotism and of the spirit world. Crandy said, "you need a Tuscarora name". I jokingly responded, "my nickname growing up was *Bong*". He laughed and said, "You are now known as Little Big Bong!".In my next book, *Race to Quantum Entanglement,* all of the magic I learned will be discussed and explained in detail.

I obtained about five hundred individual members of the Tuscarora Nation as clients. Newton referred me to an attorney in Buffalo to act as local counsel. With co-counsel and the court's permission, I could practice law in the New York jurisdiction without being admitted to the New York Bar. Having a local law firm to back me, I filed suit in November 1998 for the individual members of the Tuscarora Nation. It was the first billion-dollar lawsuit ever filed in Niagara County, New York state court. It made many state and national news outlets.

Because of the stress mixed with the Valium, I was having anger problems and other issues associated with the Valium. I had to quit. Again, I had to go through withdrawals. I had been taking

Valium continually for over a year. Not only a hassle, but it was also getting dangerous going monthly to the Mexican pharmacies with all of the gang wars along the Mexican border. I slowly reduced my intake. From four blue pills a day, I reduced my intake by one every week or so. I continued to reduce it to a fraction of a pill by cutting at first in half, then cutting into quarters. By the time I stopped completely, I was taking one tenth of a pill per day. I placed one pill in a small container on my nightstand, so I could tell myself there was one if I absolutely needed it. I never had to take that last Valium.

The withdrawal symptoms started when I reduced my dose to one pill per day. All the brazen behavior from taking the Valium rebounded to timidity during the withdrawals. I stopped eating and lost a lot of weight. The hardest withdrawal symptom was the mental tricks my mind would play. For nearly a month, I had audible hallucinations. Every word anyone spoke with an *S* would continue long after with a long drawn out *hissssssss*. It was maddening.

Another maddening symptom of withdrawal was my inability to look anyone in their eyes. No matter how hard I tried, I could not look directly into anyone's eyes. It also felt like each of my body organs reprogramed or rebooted during the withdrawal. First, my breathing pattern changed. My heart started to vibrate. I had trouble eating and sleeping. The torture of the Valium withdraw was reduced only by weed. I could not have withdrawn without Mary Jane and Crandy's concoctions. With their help, I made it through the Valium withdrawals.

I developed and worked on the case while I continued to study with Crandy and his brother after withdrawing. I conducted the discovery and responded to the defendants' discovery requests. I took those Tuscarora clients through depositions and mediation. In their mediation, three attorneys in the area attempted to mediate a settlement between my clients and the chemical companies. Both sides prepared a mediation brief. It was basically a trial brief containing all the arguments and evidence for the mediators to evaluate your case.

After the mediation panel reviewed the briefs, they heard oral arguments from both sides. Then the mediation panel made a fault determination. If the defendants' fault is greater than fifty-one percent, he is determined to be at fault. Once the fault is determined, the three-person mediation panel members each come up with an award. Each of the awards are added together and then divided by three for the average. Both parties must accept the average award to be binding. The mediation panel in the Tuscarora case made a multimillion-dollar award to the Tuscarora. It was one of the largest mediation awards in Niagara County, New York.

However, it takes two to bind the mediation award. The defendants did not accept, and the case was set for trial for nearly a year later. Several months before the trial, the tribal chiefs made a motion to intervene. They claimed Tuscarora and its people were a sovereign nation. The tribal members had no individual rights concerning tribal issues, including their individual right to sue for personal injury damages. The judge and appeals court agreed.

I was removed as the attorney for the individual members. Another law firm representing the chiefs replaced me. I worked three years on the case. I had lived at Doug's for months developing and working on the case. I had enough. I backed out of any commitments with Newton and moved back to Lansing. Several years later, I found out that the Tuscarora case settled for $720 million.

CHAPTER FOUR: JURY TRIAL LEGS

Once I moved back to Lansing, I set up an indoor grow closet. It was archaic. I used a 1000-watt high pressure sodium bulb. I lined the walls of a small closet in a basement with aluminum foil. For soil I used peat moss, sand, and other components for the growing medium. I put a vent fan in a small window at the top corner of the grow closet. I used a larger box fan to circulate the air and to help strengthen the plants. I used seeds from medium grade cannabis purchased in the area.

Even though growing, I still had sources to buy weed. The weed was pretty good if you had the money and could afford it. There were basically two types of weed available, the indoor hydroponic and the outdoor or Mexican swag. The indoor hydroponic weed was always amazing. There was White Widow, Blueberry, Skunk and Northern Lights. Hydro weed, it was called, was very expensive as it cost anywhere from three to five hundred dollars an ounce.

I might have had weed, but I did not have jury trial experience. I had tried a few multi-million-dollar cases for Newton in Texas. But got my ass kicked on all of them. I lost those cases due to lack of jury trial experience. I knew if I was ever going to hit a big win, I would have to gain a lot of jury trial experience. To gain jury trial experience, I began taking criminal court appointed cases out of Ingham and Eaton counties in Michigan. Because I was not experienced, I was appointed only to misdemeanor cases to start. I was appointed to felony cases after two years of misdemeanor trial practice. After four years, I began to get capital cases where there was a possibility of a life sentence for the defendant, my client.

Capital cases were a lot of work. I didn't like novels or books, but I was keenly fascinated with medical records, accidents, and police reports. Each case had unusual and interesting angles. I could never understand why people made the decisions to do the crime, especially against those they knew or had a relationship. I summed it up as *crack logic*. Absolutely no basis or logic for their decision. In their bent perspective, it was acceptable to do the bad deed. I kept up my quest for more experience.

Appointed attorney work brought in little money, but misdemeanors didn't take much effort or prep time. Simple assault, trespass, small drug possession or sales were the norm. I would have tried them all, but some of my appointed clients wanted to end the turmoil and plead guilty. Prosecutors often overcharged a case for negotiation purposes. My job was to reduce the possible penalties and jail time if I could not get their case dismissed. I represented those I knew were guilty and I was always willing to fight the prosecutor and the cops, guilty or not at every step. Every defendant deserved protection.

Law school did not prepare me for protecting and defending clients. If I was ever going to win criminal jury trials, I would need lots of trial experience. They called it - *jury trial legs*. It was like getting your sea legs with time and experience. Taking court appointed cases would help get me a lot of *jury trial legs*. I wanted to do as many trials as possible. I recommend my clients not to plead but to take their case to trial. I was doing on average one jury trial a month all the while trying to maintain my office caseload and trying to make enough income to pay the bills.

To gain more experience, I joined CDAM – criminal defense lawyers of Michigan. It was a statewide group of attorneys that practiced criminal law. It was a great resource for training inexperienced attorneys. Four times a year they would have a conference to train attorneys how to be great criminal defense attorneys. When I learned a trial technique at a CDAM conference, I went back and immediately performed the new technique. It was fulfilling to learn a new cross exam technique or an evidentiary objection that I immediately used in court. Cross examination was becoming my strength.

With my strong cross examination skills and techniques, two years, and fourteen jury trials later, I was ready for felony cases. After four years and twenty-one jury trials, my trial skills had sharpened, and I developed a winning record. I had my *jury trial legs*. I graduated to the most difficult cases and was appointed felony criminal sexual conduct cases, CSC. I was thrown into the perverted world of criminal sexual conduct.

One of my first appointed felony CSC cases was an animal mutilation matter in Lansing. I drove up and parked on the street side of the courthouse. The courthouse building was a seventies style building. It housed all the courts. The interior halls were marble and smelled of cleaning bleach, fear, and submission. Down the long hallway on the sixth floor was the district court's courtrooms. Down that hall was where the pre-exam conferences were held.

This was a felony criminal pre-exam conference scheduled that day for one of my appointed clients. There were felonies and misdemeanors crimes. Basically, misdemeanors carried a year or less of incarceration. While felonies carried a year or more. My client was charged with a felony. All cases, misdemeanors, and felonies, started with an investigation by the police which generated a police report. The police report was then reviewed by the prosecutor to determine if and what charges were to be filed. If charges were filed, a warrant was issued for the defendant, and he was arrested. Following arrest, an arraignment would follow wherein the charges were read to the defendant and a bond amount would be set.

After the bond is set, felony cases require a preliminary exam called probable cause hearing. The purpose of the hearing is to determine if a crime was committed and if the defendant probably committed the charged crime. If the judge found that the defendant probably committed the crime, he would *bind-over the case upstairs* to the circuit court for conclusion – trial or plea. It was a well-known proverb among criminal defense attorneys that most district court judges would bind-over up to circuit court a ham sandwich if the prosecutor requested.

After parking, I walked down the hall to the courtroom for the animal mutilation case. The assigned district judge opened his chamber door and pulled me into his office, side stepping the regular entrance into the courtroom. The judge had the police report and pictures clutched in his hands. "This is the weirdest animal mutilation case I have ever seen", he said. "They were originally looking for children".

In that weird case, three boys dressed in their *Matrix* long black coats, in July, were on the hunt for victims to sexually assault and then kill. Their interrogation further revealed they were looking for children to molest and kill but found none. However, they found some animals and birds. They chased down and caught a goose and a cat and already had a caged rabbit. They mutilated the animals while sexually assaulting the carcasses. The boys took pictures. This was a time before cameras were built into everyone's phones. Thus, the photos of their sexual mutilations were taken with a camera using film. The film had to be developed and it was dropped off at a one-day developing kiosk. The film was picked up from the kiosk and taken to the developer. A young man was the developer that day and when he processed the film, the perverted deeds were revealed. The footage was reported to police.

The boys were arrested when they picked up their photos. Foolishly, they went together to retrieve the processed film only to be arrested on the spot. They each posted bond and a pre-exam conference was set. That is what I was there that day. But none of the matrix boys appeared for their hearing. The judge canceled my client's bond, and a bench warrant was issued for him. I never heard anything more.

There was another animal cruelty defendant where I was appointed as his attorney. The police report started with the 911 call to dispatch. The caller was stunned. The witness reported that while he was delivering animal feed to a barn, he saw the defendant copulating with a horse. The crime might have gone unnoticed if the man and horse were not so loud during the act according to the witness. But the man's loud moaning and horse whimpers aroused the witness's attention. No pictures nor biological samples were taken, only the eyewitness statements. The defendant was charged and pleaded guilty with little time to serve but was ordered to a lot of psychological treatment.

The cases became more challenging. The next case was tragic. What I got from the police report was that there was a kid in the neighborhood who really wanted to impress some older gang members. He told the gang that he knew where there was a lot of weed and a lot of money. That got their attention. The leader took charge. I read in the police report stating that the leader called up his people, his posse, and talked to them about the planned *lick*. He told them to bring their guns. There was a variety of personalities and guns in that posse that he called upon. One was a minor only in tenth grade, but he had a pistol. Another defendant was a high school football star in his senior year. There were others with similar backgrounds and ages.

The gang leader got his posse with their weapons. They drove to where the boy told them the girl had the stash of weed, and cash. The gang drove in the leader's car and parked in the driveway. Breaking into the front door with their guns brandishing, they found a seventeen-year-old girl. There was no horde of cash and there certainly were no pounds of weed. The defenseless girl had just sold her car for four hundred dollars. She was growing several marijuana plants in a window planter – that was it, that was their plunder.

They took out their frustrations on the girl. The gang beat and sexually assaulted her in the house and then dragged her to the gang leader's car parked in the driveway. They threw her in the trunk. She fought back. Her screaming and struggles annoyed the gang leader so much that he ordered each member of the posse to take turns shooting her in the vaginal area with his AK-47. After several loud pops by individual gang members, the neighbors' lights turned on. The gang members scattered on foot. The brains of the operation, the gang leader, left his car, registered in his name, with the girl dying in the trunk, in the driveway. Police soon arrived and located her, but she died on the way to the hospital.

It was a no-brainer for the cops to investigate and find each of the gang members. How difficult could it be with the gang leader's car in the driveway? Once the gang leader was arrested, he spilled the beans and identified all the gang members. He cooperated for a lighter sentence. It was a court appointed case and I was assigned the football player defendant. He was the fastest of the group and darted away so quickly that none of the neighborhood witnesses could identify him. I eventually got the football player's rape, torture and murder charges dismissed for lack of any identification or evidence.

My football-star client could not leave it alone. He not only played football; he was also a budding rap artist. After his case was dismissed and he was out of jail free, he wrote, performed, and recorded a rap song, in wrap rhythm and beat, and uploaded it on YouTube. The rap song identified all the members and what they did to the girl. The wrapped lyrics explicitly described the crimes he and his fellow gang members committed. With the rapped musical confession used as a statement against him, the feds issued a warrant. Each gang member was also recharged under RICO for the murder and warrants issued for each.

My client, with all but one other gang member, was re-arrested on the federal RICO charges without incident. The one gang member who was still on the loose was driving around Lansing when the cops spotted him and attempted to apprehend him. At the conclusion of a high-speed chase, the last free gang member drove into the Red Robin's parking lot in Lansing. He ran into the Red Robin where a gun fight ensued. A pregnant server, being used as a shield by the gang member, was shot by the cops.

The whole thing, the pregnant server getting shot by the cops at Red Robbin, the break in and subsequent rape and murder of the girl was all set into motion by the girl's little brother. I didn't discover her brother's involvement until the preliminary exam. The girl was set up by her brother. He wanted to impress the gang and told them a lie about his sister's weed and money stashes. He was only twelve.

I did a torture case that I called the *sugar daddy case*. It all started when a well-to-do owner of a hardware store frequented a local strip joint in Lansing. During his frequent visits, he established a relationship with one of the dancers. The relationship soon blossomed and extended beyond the strip joint. The sugar daddy put the stripper up in a house, paid for all her bills and he gave her money for her cocaine and booze habits. The stripper had a boyfriend, and they were very content with rent covered and drug money every month.

The stripper became pregnant about the time the sugar daddy's wife discovered what was going on. She put a stop to anymore rent and drug money. That was the end of the beautiful world for the stripper and her boyfriend. They were not going to let that beautiful world slip away. The stripper and her boyfriend had a plan. The plan was to torture the stripper. While they were torturing, she would call the sugar daddy. The sugar daddy thought the stripper was carrying his child. They planned it out so that when he arrived to save the day, they would kidnap him and hold him for ransom.

The stripper's boyfriend and his brother started torturing her without calling the sugar daddy. The torturers needed weed for the torture. They called their weed dealer – my client. When he arrived with the ordered weed, he was asked, by the stripper, if he would like to assist with the torture too. My client assisted only momentarily with only a few cigarettes burns, some slaps to her breast with his hand and with that he left the torturing.

After my client left, the sugar daddy was tricked into coming over and they did attempt to kidnap him. But the plan was foiled, of course, by stupidity and crack logic. The whole plot was revealed by the sugar daddy's wife to the cops during the attempted kidnapping. All torturing participants, including the temporary torturer, my client the weed dealer, were arrested. There were three defendants each with separate trial dates and my client's trial was first. During my client's jury trial, there was a lot of testimony about the torture. One Lansing CSI investigator gave several opinions while testifying about the victim's bra and underwear. Only experts can give opinion testimony. I objected and asked if the detective was a bra expert. The judge and the jury laughed. I knew they were in my hands.

The prosecutor also helped place the jury in my hands. He put the stripper-victim on the stand to testify against my client and by doing so opened up the door for me to introduce bad habits and character evidence. Normally, I cannot discuss any bad habits or bad acts of a witness unless first brought up and introduced by the prosecutor. The prosecutor in that case foolishly asked the stripper a question during his direct exam about her cocaine use. She acknowledged the use of cocaine during her pregnancy responding to the prosecutors' questions. That was the break I needed to take advantage of the situation. I ripped her to shreds over her cocaine abuse during her pregnancy. During *void dire* I tried to load the jury with as many women with children as possible. Of the twelve-person jury, seven were women with children. I knew the ladies with kids would dislike the stripper-victim more than my client because of her use of cocaine while pregnant. I was confident I would win the case. I knew it by looking into the jurors' eyes. They were looking at me and smiling and so was this judge.

I knew it, I had a not guilty. But it was the end of the day, and the jury was released without disclosing their verdict. They were to return back the next day and their verdict would be read first thing the next morning. After the judge excused everyone and the jury was out of the room, I told my client that we were going to win, and he was going to be found not guilty. The next day, my client didn't show up. He absconded. The jury returned not *guilty in absentia*. Years later, I ran into the weed selling torturer in downtown Lansing. He told me the cops finally caught up with him four months after the trial. He was sentenced to six years for the absconding charge although he won the trial. He had won, but he lost.

CHAPTER FIVE: CHILLY

Chilly was born into a sexually perverted hell. He was sexually and physically assaulted from the day he was born. Every day, day after day he continually witnessed and was forced to participate in such base sexual perversion. Chilly's first memories were of his father sexually assaulting his siblings. Chilly's father beat his mother and his underage girlfriends, constantly forcing them to prostitute. Years of a dad forcing him to participate in assaulting his mother, dad's girlfriend, brothers, and sisters while being constantly assaulted himself. Each sexual assault was accompanied by paternal brutality. There was no hope, no one coming to save the day. A system that is supposed to protect children failed. No one came to his rescue.

Chilly's father regularly used instruments like broom sticks, shoehorns and eating utensils for his demented sexual assaults. Chilly was finally removed from the horrific environment and home-hell when he was fourteen. Not for any safety issue concerns for him, but because young Chilly himself committed sexual assaults. He was charged as a juvenile of sexual assault of young girls in similar fashion as performed by his father.

Chilly's new environment was not much better. The juvenile facilities and foster care placements were terrible as well. He was still being abused and sexually assaulted - just by different actors. When Chilly was fourteen, it was recommended by reviewing medical professionals that he should receive lifelong psychological treatment, care, prescriptive maintenance, and oversight. At sixteen, it was recommended that Chilly undergo lifelong sex offender treatment and lifelong monitoring. Those who interviewed and examined him knew then what lay ahead for Chilly and society if no intervention was in place. Of course, there was no such intervening assistance offered, no follow-up or oversight. He was just released into society.

In 2001, Chilly was sentenced to two to ten years in prison for robbing a woman of her purse, grabbing her by the throat and attempting to shove a cola bottle in her vagina. As soon as released from that charge, he committed a similar robbery and sexual assault. He was paroled twice but returned to prison. Within both probation violation allegations, Chilly sexually assaulted his victims with tree branches.

Chilly was in prison and jail on and off. In 2003 and 2004, there was a series of sexual assaults in Lansing that remain unsolved to this day. As many as twelve murders and sexual assaults correspond to those times Chilly was out on parole. They were all middle-aged and elderly women living alone. Each woman was sexually assaulted with some type of instrument. Each woman was sexually assaulted the same way. For example, the 2004 death of Barbara Tuttle, forty-five years old, was found beaten to death and sexually assaulted in a house on Washington Street, Lansing. She had also been sexually assaulted with objects. No one was charged with her murder. There were other unsolved murders.

All those unsolved similar sexually sadistic murders and no one knew there was a serial killer lurking around. Until late Saturday night and early into Sunday morning February 2005, Carolyn Kronenberg was working in her classroom preparing for the next day's Sunday class. She must have heard someone walking down the hall that night. Probably thinking it was a janitor or another professor heading home. She had no idea she about to be brutally tortured, strangled, horrifically raped, and left for dead by Michigan's most sadistic serial killer.

Carolyn Kronenberg was found bleeding and barely alive in a second-floor classroom. She had been raped, strangled, and sexually assaulted. There were electronic devices forcibly inserted into her vagina and mouth. There were bloody trails leading up and down the halls near the room where she was found. The bloody trail revealed a horrific scene of fight, submission, unconsciousness with ostensible sexual assaults continuing at intervals.

Quick to rush in, the initial investigators of the Kroonenberg murder accused Claud McCollum, black man, of committing the heinous murder. The investigation was a complete cluster fuck by everyone, and every agency involved. The cops announced they had a suspect. Their suspect was a part-time student at the same community college where Kronenberg was murdered. He was mentally slow but was determined to get a college degree. He had no fixed address and sometimes slept in college. By all accounts McCollum was a really nice guy that would always try to help out others. As is often the case, he was a young black man and that mattered.

It was like the black man accused of sexually assaulting a white woman in the movie *To Kill a Mockingbird*. The character Tom Robinson was falsely accused of raping a white girl. *To Kill a Mockingbird* was inspired by the case of the Scottsboro Boys, where nine black boys, ranging in age from thirteen to nineteen, were falsely accused of sexually assaulting two white women. Much the same in this murder case. The public didn't know it at that time though, the Prosecutor's Office and initial investigators manipulated and falsified evidence and got an innocent man convicted for the Kronenberg murder. In doing so, they allowed the murders to continue!

The investigating agencies, prosecutor's office, the judicial rubber stamping, and failures of the appointed attorney system were all to blame. From the top prosecutor to the assistant district attorneys who worked on that case. After a kangaroo trial, the young black man was sentenced to life in prison. Chilly was back in prison on a parole violation when he heard that someone else was convicted of the Kronenberg murder.

It was July 2007 and several years after Kronenberg was sexually slaughtered in her classroom late at night. With the Kronenberg murder solved, everyone thought the streets were safe again. They were wrong. After his recent parole, Chilly returned to the Lansing area, his hometown. Only after a few weeks out of prison, at-large city council member Carol Wood's mother, 76-year-old Ruth Hallman, was sexually murdered at her home in Lansing. Originally thought to be a retaliatory assault, Ms. Hallman was found dead in her front yard. That was where they found her. However, there was bloody evidence including brain matter that indicated that she had been originally attacked in her home.

It was in the Genesee neighborhood in Lansing where Ms. Hall was actively fighting against drug dealers and all of the guns. Even at her age, she was a ferocious advocate. Ms. Hall had generated enough public attention to put heat on the gangs in her neighborhood. Most Lansing knew and respected her and her daughter. Both exemplary women – doing their best to make Lansing a safe and better place.

It did not matter to Chilly that she was a good woman when he used a hammer to hit her on the side of the head. So hard that the hammer got stuck while trying to remove it from the side of Ms. Hall's head. Chilly recalled that Ms. Hall made unconscious jerky arm movements around her head while sexually assaulting her. After being incapacitated, Chilly continued to sexually assault her. It was a furious bloody assault with the hammer. She was so disfigured that not until she arrived at the hospital that it was it determined to be a sexual assault and murder. The sexual brutality of the assault with a hammer sickened even the most experienced of law enforcement.

The cops wasted no time jumping to the wrong conclusion that Ms. Hall's attackers were local gang members. The cops brought several of the gang leaders for questioning. After several days the cops finally determined that the gang members could not have done it. The last thing the gang leaders wanted was more negative attention.

The murders continued. Ms. Cooke was a recovering addict. Trying hard to stay clean. But without government assistance for rehab, it was difficult to stay clean. By all accounts she was a decent but troubled woman who made multiple attempts to withdraw from her addiction. Ms. Cooke's body was found in a seated position leaning against a tree. She had no clothing from the waist down including her shoes. There were medium sized broken-off branches inserted into her vagina and mouth. She had been tortured, strangled, and sexually assaulted. The bruising and bleeding present in those bodily areas indicated multiple insertion.

Still more murders were happening. Within two days of Ms. Cooke's murder another victim was discovered. It was 46-year-old

Debra Renfors. Ms. Renfors worked as a cook at various restaurants in Lansing including working at Michigan State University. She was a Lansing resident for over twenty years. Mrs. Renfors was a member of Eastwood Apostolic Lutheran Church, Negaunee. Her hobbies included fishing, spending time outdoors, writing poetry and she was an excellent cook. Debbie was an extremely generous person who loved helping those in need. Her memorial read:

> *Debra E. Renfors, age forty-six, a former Negaunee resident, died on Thursday, Aug. 9, 2007, at her home in Lansing, the victim of a homicide. Ms. Renfors also had battles with drug addiction. She had been off the streets for years. She was living a good, clean, and happy life when she was murdered.*

The murderer was persistent. On August 27, 2007, 64-year-old retired General Motors worker Sandra Eichorn was found stabbed to death inside her home. Sandra Eichorn was a NASCAR racing fan and Keno at Harry's Place, a popular bar on the city's west side. She'd been stabbed 36 times by a knife from her own kitchen. The vaginal area had been mutilated with a sharp object knife. Her facial area sustained multiple stab wounds. The murder site was less than a mile from where Hallman had been murdered.

The day after Eichorn's murder, Chilly knocked on Linda Jackson's door asking for work. Jackson said she didn't have any work that needed to be done but would write his information down in case she had some work for him in the future. Jackson told Chilly to stay outside by her door when she went inside to get a pen and paper to write down Chilly's name. He was told to stay outside because her dog didn't like strangers. Chilly kept looking around the street to make sure nobody was nearby when she went in to get a notepad and pencil. When she turned, he attacked her with a beer bottle. Chilly threw her to the ground smashing the beer bottle against her head and grabbing at her pants trying to pull them down. That is when her dog, Cheyanne attacked Chilly. Cheyanne, part chow, attacked Chilly viciously, saving her life. Chilly ran.

While in the hospital, Ms. Jackson told police that her attacker left his name. The search was on. The news broke into the afternoon's regularly televised programs and announced there was a suspect. The cops spread across the city. Later, a man fitting

Chilly's description was spotted on a downtown sidewalk. The cops descended like flies upon the area of the sighting. Chilly was spotted and arrested right there on the street.

Chilly was apprehended August 28, 2007. The same night he was arrested, I got a phone call. It was from a young lady that I represented on a marijuana charge earlier that year. I had her charges dismissed. I recognized her voice immediately. I could hear her take a nervous big breath and say, "the man they arrested today for all those murders was my brother". I did not know what to say at first. She asked if I would represent him. I agreed to meet her, Chilly's cousins and the rest of the family the next day. I was to meet them at my office in Okemos, Michigan, a Lansing suburb. I had been at that office location since I moved back from Texas. I had an office share arrangement therewith several other attorneys. We shared the costs of utilities, secretarial staff, and library. We ate what we killed, meaning and we did not share clients or income.

I met Chilly's sister and cousins at my shared office. They explained to me Chilly's harsh and abusive history growing up. If he was guilty, they wanted to make sure he was treated fairly and safely. There had also been threats made against Chilly and his family. I was going to get involved and I decided to represent Chilly's.

After telling me about the threats, they further explained that they did not have much money. No savings, no investments. but they had a cup of old coins that was passed down through the family. The cup of old coins was their retainer. I later had the coins valued at $282; I took one of Michigan's biggest criminal cases for a cup of old coins.

I went to see Chilly at the Ingham County Jail the next morning before his arraignment. I had been in and out of that jail house for years representing clients of all sorts. I knew most of the jailers and jail staff there. Being recognized by the jail staff or deputies did not give any defense attorney benefits or granted any special slack. Cops called defense attorneys *mouth pieces*. That's a derogatory slang word to most criminal defense attorneys. Court appointed attorneys were the lowest to cops. Defense attorneys were ignored and often made to wait unnecessarily for hours to see their appointed client. Defense attorneys would meet with clients in rooms locked-from-the-outside. If there was ever an altercation or fight with a client, the staff would take their sweet ass time to come and assist. That's why I always carried a large metal pen – to stab a mother fucker in the eye if they tried to get at me.

I met with Chilly that next morning with my pen in my shirt pocket. He was wearing a paper gown. He was being held under a suicide watch. There was a special section of the jail for those under suicide watch. The suicide part of the jail cells was right in the booking area so that the suicidal inmate could be watched. I walked into his cell. He was sitting in his paper gown. He did not look like a crazed serial killer. He was soft spoken. Not threatening at all. I asked about his interrogation and how was being treated. He told me that after asking for an attorney many times, the police beat his ass to get a confession out of him. The newspaper reported:

> Chilly, 27, of Lansing, was ordered held without bond during his video arraignment in Lansing District Court. Chilly, a recent prison parolee, was handcuffed and wearing an orange jail jumpsuit while standing beside his attorney, Mike O'Briant.

Chilly waived the right to have a preliminary examination within fourteen days to get the preliminary exam reset. That would give me more time to prepare for the monstrous preliminary exam. I needed it. Newspapers reported:

> After the arraignment, Chilly's family members declined comment to the media and referred questions to his lawyer. Macon's state of mind was good, O'Briant said, adding that he will seek a referral for a psychiatric evaluation. He's incompetent, look at his history, O'Briant said. O'Briant also plans to file a motion to change venue, citing public statements about the case made by the Lansing mayor and police chief.

While I was preparing for Chilly's preliminary exam, the Lansing police, the Michigan State Police, and the Lansing City Mayor, were all making statements about the case to the press. I petitioned the court for a gag order to prevent any further disclosure of the case to the press. The judge granted my request and issued a restraining order preventing law enforcement officials and prosecutors from speaking publicly about certain aspects of the case. I also petitioned to suppress the dissemination of those parts of the arrest warrants not available to the public that had details about the case and my client.

Several days after granting my request for the gag order, a Michigan State Trooper spoke to a reporter and disclosed certain information about the similarities in the murders thereby violating the gag order. The reporter wrote an article disclosing what the trooper told her. I immediately filed a motion to show cause. I was asking the court to hold the trooper and the Michigan State Police in criminal and civil contempt for violating the gag order.

The state trooper was represented by the Michigan Attorney General's office. One of the attorney general's assisting attorneys handled the case. However, there was no defense for them against the violation. I subpoenaed the reporter to come to court and testify. She testified that the trooper disclosed, telling her in person, restricted information that was later included in her newspaper article. The reporter confirmed that the trooper made the statements just days after the judge issued the gag order. The judge granted my motion and held the trooper in criminal contempt and ordered him to pay five thousand dollars to me for the fragrant violation. Any jail time was waived. After the hearing, the assistant attorney general said threateningly, "someday either the Michigan State Police or the AG will get payback". I replied, "Fuck you. All I was doing was representing my client zealously". I still cringe when I see a Michigan State Trooper.

The preliminary exam was a scientific review of the evidence collected by the CSI team. There were pathologists and medical doctors. They testified about the time and manner of death. Each of the two murders were sexually horrific even from the pathologist's point of reference. There was also DNA evidence. The Michigan State Police have a lab in Lansing. The DNA cultures and testing were performed there. Their DNA expert was an old guy in a white suit.

I was lucky enough to be granted a DNA expert after much complaining. Chilly would not get a fair trial without experts to assist. Experts are used to give opinion testimony in a particular area of expertise. I gained experience employing experts in Newton's cases. In Newton's mass action cases, there would be a long list of experts. Some include epidemiologists, wind molders, medical doctors, engineers, and mathematicians among many others. If the witness did not have direct knowledge, they generally could not give an opinion about some nuance assumption in the case. The circuit court judge granted my request for the state to pay for Chilly's experts. However, the judge would not grant my request for compensation and get paid by the county. Though routinely appointed to murder cases, the judge would not allow me to get paid.

At least I was appointed a DNA expert. I used a headhunting firm that provided forensic experts in different fields. I was assigned a DNA expert, that until only recently had worked for the Michigan State Police. She had been fired for testing her husband's underwear without authorization for evidence of her his infidelity. When her husband's unauthorized test results came back guilty, she complained about the results. He reported her unauthorized use of state equipment for personal use. She was fired immediately.

The DNA expert had a history of sorts with this case. She was working for the state when the initial DNA testing was done in the Corolyn Kronenberg murder. She oversaw the testing and opined on the results. She voiced her concerns that there was no link to McCollum. She was ignored. There was no evidence to connect McCollum to the Kronenberg slaughter. There was DNA evidence left behind, but not McCollum's. She noted that there was no biological evidence on McCollum's clothing. No blood, no bodily fluids at all were discovered on his clothing. The investigators would not listen, she said. They were hell bent on prosecuting someone, even if it's the wrong person. There was exculpatory evidence and lack of DNA evidence, yet the prosecutor pressed on against McCollum knowing full well that there was no evidence linking McCollum. He just did not do it, she repeated.

In Chilly's case, the DNA expert examined the lab work and results performed by the state police lab. There was no doubt that Chilly's DNA was located at each murder scene, but she disclosed that there was an 'unknown" donor DNA sample at some of the murder scenes. She said that the unknown donor had nearly the same DNA pattern as Chilly's. DNA testing results were measured by thirteen markers. The DNA expert said that the unknown donor shared seven of the same markers and therefore must be a close relative of Chilly's. Their DNA markers differed slightly. She said it could be a brother, cousin or even his dad that left biological fluids along with Chilly's at the murder scenes. Chilly's Dad was still alive, and Chilly had a couple of brothers. One brother, Hobbs, was in jail for felonious assault and was awaiting his trial in the same county jail as Chilly. He had not nor ever been charged with any of the murders. The cops would never comprehend that there were two serial killers.

It freaked me out to get high while I was working on Chilly's case. All of the information, photos, and statements about the murder, would combine to give me a 3D view of the crime scenes. It must have triggered flashbacks from all of the LSD, because every time I was high, I would transport to the crime scene as it was occurring.

The preliminary exam was held about two months after the arraignment. That much time was needed for the prosecutor to obtain and provide all the records pertaining to the cases. The prosecutor is required by law to disclose any relevant and exonerating evidence to the defendant's attorney. Failure to do so might result in a mistrial or complete dismissal of the charges. After the preliminary exam, which in this case lasted two weeks, the trial was set.

The trial was set months away from the prelim. The chief judge appointed himself as the trial attorney. The chef judge was a bully. His decisions depended on his mood of the day or if the plaintiff or defendant was a good-looking girl. One day the judge's dog ran off. I could overhear him yelling at his wife blaming her for the dog's escape. He was always condescending to me, but that was nothing unusual for most judges. Three months before the trial, the judge had me and the prosecutor in his chambers going over prospective jury list and the jury questionnaires. I went to the judge's chambers every day in the afternoon for several weeks, tweaking the prospective jury pool list and proposed jury instructions. While in his chambers, we got to hear the judge piss and moan about everything.

The trial was soon to start. While visiting Chilly several times per week, I began to visit his brother, Hobbs. My visits with Hobbs were undocumented. There was no record of me ever meeting him. I roamed the jail inner halls freely. I met with whomever I wanted without a record of my visiting them once I had already checked in for a different inmate. I was preparing Hobbs as a *take the fifth* witness for Chilly's trial. However, use of a *take the fifth* witness required a twenty-four-hour notice to the prosecutor that the prospective witness will decline to answer some questions because it may tend to self-incriminate.

My plan was to have Chilly's brother testify in his defense. Hobbs was going to testify about Chilly's abuses at the hands of their father. But my big plan was to have Chilly's brother take the stand as a witness to confuse the jury. I wanted to the jury to ask themselves why Hobbs wasn't arrested and prosecuted for the murders too and to ask themselves whether the prosecutor charged the wrong person again. So much confusion that my motion for a mistrial might be granted. I planned to put Hoggs on the stand. I was going to show him the DNA reports and ask him if it was his DNA that was also found at the crime scene. His brother would have to decline to answer because it may tend to self-incriminate.

There were multiple eyewitnesses who created artist renditions of possible murder suspects. None of the witness-based sketches resembled Chilly. Chilly was short, stocky, and dark complected. His brother Hobbs was tall, thin and had a lighter complexion. Some of the witnesses said they saw a man on a bicycle in the areas near the time of the murders. Up on the stand, I planned to put the drawing right next to his face in front of the jury and ask if that was him. He would have to take the fifth again.

Chilly did not have a bike and was known to walk and take the bus everywhere while his brother always rode a bike. I would establish that his brother rode a bike everywhere. Even to the murder scenes, I was going to ask him. He would be forced again to respond by taking the fifth. That was my plan and that is what Hobbs and I practiced during our clandestine meeting - that was my trial strategy. Chilly, his case, and I were in the news constantly. I saw myself in an interview on the noon news and then I the evening, there would be a different report or interview about Chilly all over the state and some national news outlets as well.

The high publicity trial was finally about to begin. With any jury trial, the first phase is called *voir dire* meaning speak the truth. This is at the beginning of the trial when the jury is picked. There are twelve jury members with two extra jurors making fourteen in the jury box. The alternatives are chosen from the jury pool to act as extras just in case an original juror gets sick or has to be excused for some other reason. In Chilly's case, there were over two hundred prospective jurors in the gallery.

The court was called to order and the judge read a few court rules to the prospective jurors in the gallery. Once properly admonished by the court, the prosecutor and criminal defense attorney begin their *voir dire*. The prosecutor always goes first. Both sides ask questions to determine if any of the jurors are biased or have preconceived notions about the case. Jurors may be dismissed by the court, prosecutor, or defense attorney challenge.

Neither the prosecutor or defense attorney may unilaterally dismiss any juror using a peremptory challenge. With a peremptory challenge, the attorney can dismiss a juror for no reason at all. In a murder case, each attorney is allowed twelve preemptory challenges. Another way to dismiss a prospective juror was for cause. One must be able to argue and explain to the judge why a certain prospective juror is unfit for duty to be dismissed by the judge for cause. It can be used if a juror is blatantly biased. The prospective juror may also be excused for cause if they are related or in a relationship with one of the parties or witnesses. If a juror has been in a similar type of trial, he may be excused for cause. Strikes for cause excuses are unlimited. Benton Musslewhite excelled by getting entire jury pools dismissed for cause alone.

In Chilly's case, I asked one of the prospective jurors if he assumed my client was guilty because he was black. That hopeful juror responded that yes, he believed my client was guilty because he was black and sitting at the defendant's table. Before asking the judge to excuse him for cause, I roasted him with embarrassing questions about his racial motivations. *Voi dire* is also where an experienced attorney will subliminally educate the jury on the theory of the case. In my void dire, I hinted at the testimony to be given by a special witness - Hobbs. I hinted also to the jury that the police rushed this investigation just as they rushed to conclusion in the Kronenberg murder case.

After *voir dire* came the opening statements. The prosecutor went first. Each side explained their theory of the case, introduced the exhibits and witnesses and their expected testimony. It was my strategy to interrupt and confuse the prosecutor during his opening statement by making objections. It was never difficult to find something objectionable. The prosecutor would invariably give a personal opinion, such as: I believe this defendant is guilty; or I believe the defendants' attorney is wrong. At no time can either attorney insert their personal feelings and beliefs in any of their statements. A well-placed objection during the prosecutors opening always knocks them off track.

The prosecutor always went first with their opening statement. After the prosecutor's opening statement, it was my turn. The judge asked me, "Mr. O'Briant, do you have an opening statement?" I was looking at the ground and purposefully ignoring him. He raised his voice a little louder, "Mr. O'Briant, are you going to give an opening statement?' I still ignored him. He was angry and yelled, "Mr. O'Briant, do you have an opening or not?" I immediately jumped up and did my best George Carlin rendition of the seven words you can't say in public, "shit, piss, fuck, cunt, cock sucker, mother fucker and tits". The judge fell back in his chair. Looking over at the jury, I said "ladies and gentlemen of the jury, if any of those words hurt your feelings, wait till you get into the facts of this case". I continued with my opening to further explain my opposition to the prosecutor's witnesses. I also mentioned my special witness - Hobbs.

After the opening statement of the prosecutor and me, the prosecutor presented his case against Chilly. I objected continually to the quality of witnesses and their lack of any scientifically approved opinions. I argued that the prosecution brought in every kind of crackpot expert. I objected vehemently, yet every objection was denied. I made over one hundred or so objections during the trial. The prosecution finished her case in record time – two days for two murders and a felonious assault. On the third day it was my turn to present evidence to the jury. I had promised the jury a witness that would explain everything. I was up first and going to put Hobbs on the stand the next morning.

I arrived early to court the next morning to prepare for my star witness's testimony. Being early, I expected the courtroom to be empty. When I walked in, however, the judge was already on the bench. Below and next to him was the prosecutor. He was the elected prosecutor and the person voted into office. Standing next to him was a Michigan State trooper with the look of a lifetime of steroid use. The judge summoned me up to the bench. I noticed a grin on all their faces. Standing in front of the judge, he warned me that if I called Chilly's brother to the stand as a witness, he would instruct the state trooper to immediately tackle "and beat my ass in front of the jury and then I will charge you with witness intimidation".

The time between giving notice and that morning, they had gotten to Chilly's brother. I was required to give a 24-hour notice to the prosecutor that my witness would take the *Fifth* while questioned on the stand. They got to him. The cops threatened to charge him with all the murders if he did not cooperate with them. They told Hobbs to say that I asked him to lie. I thought about taking an ass kicking in front of the jury, but I remembered that Chilly wanted kill again. I also had a trip planned as soon as the trial was over. I pondered about what to do.

The jury was brought in. The judge asked if I had any witnesses. I said "no witnesses your honor" in a shameful tone. The prosecutor was then instructed to give her closing statement. I then gave a halfhearted unprepared closing statement. The jury looked bewildered. "Where was Chilly's special witness", they must have been thinking. The jury was out less than an hour for deliberation. Guity was the verdict. Another Kangaroo trial with my help. The verdict should have been guilty by reason of insanity. I was hoping for a mistrial so I could get another chance at an insanity determination and again argue that Chilly was incompetent to stand trial.

Sentencing was scheduled several months after the trial. A

presentence report was prepared by the probation department. The presentence report covered Chilly's horrific life, criminal history, work history and sentencing recommendation. It was void of the specialists' earlier warnings from Chilly's past. Chilly's presentence report was a book, however. Michigan uses sentencing guidelines to determine the length of jail sentence. Working through calculated enhancers, the defendant is given two numbers. The low and high end of the guidelines are set as the defendant's particular minimum and maximum prison sentence. Many variables are factored into the guidelines such as: criminal history, was a gun used or violence perpetrated. The age of the victim is another variable. Each category has a coordinating number. The numbers are added up and then applied to a graph. The graph shows, when the numbers are triangulated, the minimum and maximum prison.

Chilly got the maximum sentence of life without the possibility of parole. I argued he should have been found not guilty by reason of insanity. Chilly was never charged with the other murders. He was not charged with the Kronenberg or Hall murders. Chilly never faced charges in the deaths of Barbra Tuttle, Ruth Hallman, Deborah Cooke, Debra Renfors or Karen Yates. There were other victims too that were sexually assaulted and murdered that fit the same pattern, but again, he was never charged nor was any other effort made to investigate Chilly's involvement.

Chilly's story was not finished. In 2016, the elected prosecutor, the prosecutor in Chilly's and the Kronenberg trials, was charged with pandering, engaging a prostitute and willful neglect of duty. He was originally charged with more serious crimes relating to his forcing women who had pending criminal charges to perform sexual favors in return for leniency. He was offered to do just one year in a neighboring county jail in return for pleading guilty.

Michigan's Governor, Gretchen Whitmer was appointed during this time as the temporary head prosecutor at Ingham County Prosecutor's office after the removal and criminal conviction of her predecessor. She was appointed just long enough to oversee the plea deal and to make sure the plea agreement was carried out. The disgraced prosecutor received less than one year in jail for his criminal acts. He was never held accountable for the criminal and wrongful conviction of the McCollum in the Kronenberg debacle. If Chilly had been apprehended sooner, there would not have been innocent women slaughtered.

CHAPTER SIX: ENBRIDGE: THE LARGEST OIL SPILL ON THE NORTH AMERICAN CONTINENT

In 2008 Michigan voters approved medical marijuana. Weed had a new name in Michigan – CANNABIS. It was legal if you were a medical marijuana patient. It didn't take much to get a medical marijuana card. Just had to pay a doctor and then get certified. I no longer had to search for weed and having to take whatever was available at whatever price demanded. You never knew who grew it or what pesticides and fertilizers were being used. Under Michigan law, all retail cannabis had to be tested for strength and contaminants. There was such a great selection and variety of safe cannabis. Times were different.

The music was different too. I felt like Rip Van Winkle with the new music of the times. I heard alien sounds coming from Lady Gaga, Eminem, Snoop Dog, and others on the radio. I still listened to the classics like The Doors, Led Zepplin, Styx, Frank Zappa, Black Sabbath, and Deep Purple. I liked old Jamaican dub like Burning Spear, Eek-a-Mouse and The Mighty Three.

In Lansing, dispensaries popped up overnight up and down Michigan Avenue. It was a boom for the grow shops too. There were farmers cannabis markets on the weekends. Everyone started to grow cannabis then. Under the new Michigan Medical Marijuana laws, once certified, a medical marijuana patient could buy and possess up to two- and one-half ounces of Cannabis. A patient could also appoint a caregiver. The caregiver could grow twelve plants per patient with a limit of five patients. If a caregiver was a patient too, he could grow legally up to seventy-two plants.

It was great – anyone with a certification could grow cannabis legally and it was 2010. President Obama was in office. The big earthquake hit Haiti. Google was infected by a massive cyber-attack. The Tea Party movement was gaining momentum. The Winter Olympics were held in Vancouver. Texting while driving laws started to appear in some of the states. A SeaWorld trainer was attacked and dragged to her death by a killer whale. In April, the Deep-Water Horizon well exploded in the Gulf of Mexico and became the worst environment disaster ever.

The BP oil spill was on my mind during a criminal court appearance that morning. I was appointed to a man who was caught using a hidden camera to film his daughter in the bathroom. I could never understand why people do what they do. After the hearing, I went to my office, worked on a brief all afternoon, and then went home to work on my indoor grow.

It was that evening on July 7, 2010, and it happened – THE ENBRIDGE PIPELINE OIL SPILL. I heard the special announcement about the Enbridge crude oil pipeline spill. The location was just forty-five minutes from my office in Lansing. The first reports downplayed the spill by Enbridge disclosing that only several hundred gallons of simple crude oil had been spilled. It was only out of precaution that some families were asked to evacuate. A breach in the Enbridge pipeline occurred in a piece of pipe over Tallmadge Creek near a little berg called Ceresco. Ceresco was only a few miles from Battle Creek. Talmadge Creek fed into the Kalamazoo River. The Kalamazoo River ran through Battle Creek and emptied directly into Lake Michigan.

The Enbridge pipeline oil spill occurred near Marshal Michigan. If the pipeline spill had occurred in Texas, it would be a lawyers' field day. It was just like when I had the KFC client sign-up field day in Corpus Christi years earlier. If this happened along the Texas gulf coastline, the roads to Marshall would be clogged with lawyers and case runners feasting on the thousands of possible clients. Case runners are non-attorneys that go around after a mass accident incident and illegally solicit clients for attorneys. It was an illicit solicitation for legal service that they performed. Runners would, once they obtained a lot of signatures, sell the clients and their executed contracts to lawyers. They may be working for an attorney, or they could be independent, either way, it was an unethical and illegal practice. Such runners worked well in minority neighborhoods in Texas.

The lawyers in the Valley had it all tied up. They were an airtight runner solicitation cartel in the Valley around Brownsville and Harlingen that I could never break into. Every accident in the Vally attracted swarms of runners. Such a large event like the Enbridge oil spill, if in Texas, attorneys and their case runners would have been out setting up shop in abandoned houses or just soliciting, illegally, directly out of their cars to sign up prospective clients. Like flies on shit.

I did not hear of or see any attorneys or runners rushing in for the Enbridge spill. I kept waiting to hear that some law firm out of Detroit had filed a suit. Five days had gone by and still no news of any litigation. I considered whether to get involved and whether to pursue the case. I thought to myself "Fuck, another chemical release disaster just after BP in the Gulf of Mexico". It made me mad because this time the spill occurred in my backyard. However, I was very hesitant to get involved. I was still licking my wounds from the Tuscarora and Macon debacles. It was foreboding - this case would be a disaster if I got involved.

It was bigger than me and my capabilities to manage it. I just had to do something though. No one else was suing. I thought to myself, "hell, the EPA hadn't even made it out yet - all those people and the kids exposed". The EPA didn't start monitoring until the fifth day after the spill occurred. All those affected for life now after being subjected to all those carcinogens. Many of the crude oil compounds were very volatile at those hot summer temperatures. It meant that all the harmful compounds would evaporate into the air and spread over the populated areas.

The oil in the Enbridge pipeline was a thick petroleum crude which would have a significant effect on humans and in cleaning it up. I knew from previous crude oil disasters in Corpus Christi that many of the volatile crude oil compounds were carcinogenic, especially benzene. Those compounds evaporate quickly but not before exposing those in the vicinity. If not monitored and measured right then, there would be no evidence of the high levels of carcinogens ever being released. No Detroit firm had filed yet.

I was not sure why no one else had filed a lawsuit. Newton taught me, "Filing suit quickly preserves the evidence and allows for an immediate investigation, otherwise you will lose important evidence that otherwise could be destroyed by the defendants". A lot of evidence could already have been deteriorated, missing, and gone. No one was suing - nothing was being done. The amount of crude oil released in the Enbridge oil spill would only be outdone, as later discovered, by the BP oil well explosion in the Gulf that occurred just a few months earlier. No one knew it at the time, nonetheless, that the Enbridge oil spill would be the largest oil spill disaster on the North American continent. The magnitude of poisonous types of chemicals released would affect those exposed for the rest of their life.

I knew the case would require a lot of time and expense money. I had some time, but not the finances, to properly maintain the case. But I could not bear the thought that Enbridge might get away with unless someone, anyone sued them immediately. I thought to myself, "I had taken on other cases by the seat of my pants, why not this one. I could file the lawsuit and maybe get financing or an easy settlement". I was lying to myself. There were never any quick settlements or easy lawsuits. "My experience is that most chemical exposure mass action cases take up to five or more years to finalize and only one in four of those cases are successful", warned Newton in the Texas cases. But something had to be done. I did not want to take on such a burden. I anxiously waited to hear of a lawsuit or any litigation at all. None!

It was not going to turn out good, but I could not sit around and watch. Six days after the spill, I ran an advertisement in the Battle Creek Enquirer soliciting for exposure victims to the spill. I received a call from a lady named Betty the day after the advertisement was placed. She lived in a mobile home park in Battle Creek, Michigan that was surrounded on three sides by the Kalamazoo River. Betty's double wide was encircled along with all those who lived in the trailer park with her in Battle Creek.

Battle Creek had a creepy and slightly bigoted past. Historically, Battle Creek had an unusual indigenous history which helped give its name. Battle Creek is located at the joining of the Kalamazoo and Battle Creek rivers. It was nicknamed Cereal City for being the Kellogg Company's founding city. The town had a dark history after a brutal encounter by government officials on members of the Potawatomi tribe in 1824. Some members of the tribe were starving and approached the officials' camp asking for food because the U.S. Army was late delivering supplies to the reservation as required under their treaties. The government officials shot and killed, like dogs, many of the starving Potawatomi as they tried to steal food. That's the big battle Battle Creek is named after.

Dr. Kellogg, a founder of the cereal company, created another dark cloud over Battle Creek. He created the Kellogg's Race Betterment Foundation. It was an openly bigoted organization that supported a *separate but equal* philosophy. This led citizens of color to being subjected to unwarranted police harassment. Racial housing covenants were in full force keeping black families out of white neighborhoods. Blacks were prevented from working in the local schools or city institutions and not allowed to hold any significant positions or posts in the city's corporate or public sector. Because of Battle Creek's historical past and current bigotry, Dr. Martin Luther King, Jr. held a rally and spoke there against the prevalent discrimination. So did Senator Humphrey, President Johnson, and the then heavyweight champion of the world, Muhammad Ali and all spoke in opposition to the city's bigotry.

I was not aware of Battle Creek's tainted history when I drove out to meet Betty. It was a Sunday, over a week since the initial spill began. Being summer, the poisonous volatile compounds from the spill were still hanging in the air, but not nearly at the level during the initial release. As I drove into Battle Creek, I could smell sickly-sweet and acrid petroleum vapors. It was intense. The fumes burnt breathing in and with a chemical after taste on exhale. I could not get away from it. It settled on clothes, unprotected skin and absorbed by my lungs. The nasty fumes became stronger as I drove to the Betty's mobile home park.

Next to Betty's trailer lot, there was an empty lot where on the ground were strewn dead black birds. Not crows but smaller birds. It looked like they dropped out of the sky and fell on the ground in the same pattern. An ominous tip of the iceberg of the overall effects of the massive spill. There were men women, children, families, couples, and older folks that were there, standing around to meet me at Betty's. The trailer park was made up of very grungy mobile homes and some had been around for fifty years. It was not a plush trailer park by any means. Betty's place was the nicest of them all. She lived in the only double wide trailer in the park. I pulled into Betty's driveway ready to meet them all about a possible mass action lawsuit against Enbridge.

Mass action chemical exposure cases are like plays where the characters are played by the clients in an all too familiar script. Battle Creek was the stage, and my clients were the current actors in every repeating scenario. With my experience, that community spokesperson will eventually turn on me and attempt to hijack the case later. Newton warned me of this phenomenon. He must have faced it over a hundred times. He included in his written mass action retainer contracts safeguards in his contract to protect him against the spokesperson's takeover. Those recalcitrant clients always wanted more of the settlement money because of their assistance. I knew Betty would be an adversary in the future. The group leader always files a grievance and complains that they did not get a fair share of the settlement.

Besides the group leader part, there were other parts to be played as well in the mass action lawsuit theater. Every case had someone playing the part of the community rabblerouser and agitator. Agitators would attend all the Enbridge public explanation meetings with their entourage. Always causing a scene, taking pictures and videos, and protesting for self-aggrandizement at every chance. Rabblerousers ultimately intimidate, coerce, and secretly demand black mail type payments.

I was ready for the actors and the parts they were to play in the Enbridge lawsuit. I drove through part of the mobile home park to get to Betty's doublewide. The mobile homes looked old and so too did the inhabitants look worn out too. It was that way before the pipeline spill. When I got out of my car I was ushered in by Betty. The crowd stayed outside while Betty, her husband, her older son, and I discussed the case and my possible representation. I told them about my experiences. I explained that she must act quickly, or a lot of the necessary evidence would not be retrievable. She told me of what happened.

She told me none of the trailer park households were asked or ordered to evacuate. Betty and her husband were sitting in the living room when a noxious fumes began to seep into their mobile home. "The fumes struck me immediately and it was nauseating. My head started hurting, instant headache and my eyes got itchy and started to watering". Betty continued, "I ran outside thinking it might be a gas leak inside, but it was worse outside". Betty and her husband had to shelter-in-place, as erroneously advised, because like so many others in the trailer park, they did not have the money to stay in a hotel. They, and most of the others in the trailer park, just stuck it out. I was there a week after the oil spill and the fumes were almost unbearable. I could not imagine how bad it was right after the spill.

The local county health department told a select few in more affluent neighborhoods to leave their homes and take their pets to shelters. Finally, days after the spill, the county officials publicly issued a meager advisory against drinking either city or well water. I was never quite sure why they did not order a complete evacuation for everyone in the affected in the area. Volatile organic carcinogenic compounds were detected when the testing equipment was finally set up by the EPA and by the state days later. Five days after the release had ceased, benzene was still detected in the air at dangerous levels - five days later! Only a few families were relocated and provided bottled water. There was nowhere to go anyway, all the hotels were filled.

The spill happened in Marshall, Michigan. At least two million gallons of sand tar crude oil, thinned with benzene blackened more than two miles of Talmadge Creek and almost thirty-six miles of the Kalamazoo River. About 150 families were permanently relocated and most of the tainted stretch of river between Marshall and Kalamazoo remained closed to the public for years.

The disaster was triggered by a tear in the pipeline operated by Enbridge. It was the most expensive oil pipeline spill ever. Despite the scope of the damage, the Enbridge spill didn't attract much national attention because it occurred days after oil stopped spewing from BP's well in the Gulf of Mexico, which had ruptured three months earlier. Early reports about the Enbridge spill also downplayed its seriousness, especially about the large amounts of benzene release. Just about everybody, including the EPA officials who rushed to Marshall, did not know of the benzene.

The EPA didn't know then that the Enbridge pipeline was carrying bitumen, the dirtiest, stickiest crude oil on the market. Bitumen is so thick—about the consistency of peanut butter—that it doesn't flow from a well like the normal liquid crude oil flowing in US petroleum pipelines. Bitumen crude oil is thinned with large quantities of benzene, a known human carcinogen. I did not know about the unusually large amount benzene either at first. Enbridge kept it to themselves. After meeting Betty and the others in the trailer park, I jumped in with both feet. I rented an office in Battle Creek, hired a secretary, and bought some furniture. Soon I had people scheduled to come in to review their paperwork.

From that first meeting with Betty, I obtained 420 mobile home residential clients. They consisted of men, women, and children. I filed a lawsuit the next day, eight days after the spill, in the Calhoun County Circuit Court. I included an expedited motion for an injunction to freeze and preserve all of Enbridge's records both on paper and electronically. Newton would be proud of the quick legal moves. Along with the lawsuit and motion for injunctions, I also served discovery requests including requests for production and interrogatories. I hit them with everything.

A week after hitting them with the lawsuit, discovery requests and motions upon Enbridge, I was served with forty-five banker boxes full of Enbridge's responses to the lawsuit and their responses to my discovery demands. I also received their requests for documents, interrogatories, and notices of depositions for each of my four hundred and twenty clients, including the children. I immediately felt the heavy weight of the case fall on my shoulders. I panicked.

I panicked because of all the work and effort that would be required to respond to all of Enbridge's discovery requests. I had to respond to interrogatories in twenty-one days or have my case dismissed. The interrogatories questions ask the basics, such as, name, address, phone number and basic personal history. The interrogatories also asked personal questions about their damages, their claims made in the lawsuit and their medical and criminal history. Normally each set of interrogatories was thirty to forty questions. Those questions have multiple subparts. It was quite a daunting undertaking when you consider the sheer number of questions that must be processed and responded to by me formally. Responding to the mountain of discovery requests and the associated work is the most difficult part of any chemical exposure mass action case. Once I received the responses, all that information had to be processed. Thus, I had boxes and boxes to go through and process. I got everything done on time, just barely. The depositions and discovery went on through the next year.

During the next summer there was a violent thunderstorm in Battle Creek. It whipped up a small tornado that hit the trailer park destroying many of my clients' trailers. Devastating at least half of them and damaging everyone's property to some degree, many of my clients were forced to move out. I lost track of some of them by the time the holidays rolled around.

It was Christmas and I was down to 353 remaining clients in the Enbridge lawsuit. Many of the remaining clients had not recovered from the tornado from earlier that year. It was no secret that most of my clients were in a tough financial spot. Enbridge made a strategic offer to settle just when my clients were at their weakest. They were poor and some of them had no place to live after the tornado. Enbridge took full advantage of their situation, their financial hardships, and predicaments, offering only a pittance of what was my clients' real and actual personal damages. It was an insult to me and my remaining clients. Every one of my clients was exposed to large amount of benzene and other carcinogens. There was a considerable chance that with the high levels of benzene, many of my clients would develop cancer in the future. But Enbridge offered only $400 to each adult and less for the children. As their attorney, even though I loathed the offer, I was ethically obligated to disclose the terrible offer to them. I was out a lot of time and money if they accepted the messily offer. Against my recommendations and pleas, just like dominos, all my clients toppled over each other and fell into the arrogantly small settlement.

    Most all my clients demanded that accept Enbridge's offer and settle. There were a few clients that held out. The hard part was getting the holdouts to sign off and agree to settle on the amount offered. Invariably, there were some who expected to be paid more because they thought their injuries were greater, or they assisted with the case and deserve more money. They were just following the script. But with a lot of work, I was able to get everyone to sign off on the crappy settlement. I knew from the beginning, when contemplating my entry into the Enbridge oil spill case, that it would not end well for me. I just had to step in and get my ass kicked - again.

CHAPTER SEVEN: STUXNET AND PANAMA

The first Enbridge lawsuit was not a complete loss. During the first Enbridge lawsuit, the trailer park suit that just settled for pennies, I continued to sign new clients for a second, much larger lawsuit. I gathered about two thousand new clients who suffered exposures from the same Enbridge oil spill. The second case was growing exponentially and already bigger than me. I needed help. I decided to contact Newton. I had not spoken to him in almost ten years. I called him and set an appointment with him for the following week.

That next week, I flew to Houston from Detroit. I knew the best way to catch him alone and to be waiting for him at his office parking lot early in the morning. I took the last flight out of Detroit to Houston. I got into Houston about one in the morning. I rented a car at the airport and drove to Newton's compound. I brought some weed and smoked it on the way to Newton's office. I pulled into Newton's parking lot around 2:30 a.m. I parked and slept in my car for a while and then was up and ready for Newton when he drove up in his old beater. The large gate to his compound opened. He pulled into the driveway and then into his compound. I startled him a little when I jumped out of my car and yelled at him. Once he realized who it was, he smiled and motioned me to come into his compound. He looked surprised to see me, especially at that time in the morning.

Newton and I entered his compound and went up to his private restaurant. His staff had already prepared his breakfast for him and had it waiting. I ordered breakfast as well and we discussed the Enbridge case. Newton was concerned about the lack of any serious injuries. "Those type of injuries, sore throats, itchy runny eyes, headaches, and nausea, they are not very serious injuries. Too bad no one died". Newton continued sarcastically, "then you would have a great case. You sure got taken to the cleaners on your first suit against Enbridge".

Even with his reservations, he agreed to investigate and take a look at the Enbridge case. He told me he would get back to me in a week or two. "Hey, you are still up in Michigan", he asked as I was about to leave. "I have a big case that was transferred from California to Michigan's federal court jurisdiction. The cases are out of Panama, central America, and concern a group of indigenous banana plantation worker near the Coast Rican border in Panama. You got along OK with all those Tuscarora Native Americans in New York. Why don't you help these Native Americans out too?"

I flew back to Michigan after meeting with Newton pondering the Panama scenario. When I arrived back in Michigan, a mother whose daughter was shot by police was asking for help. Her daughter was black, mentally handicapped, and about twenty-five years old. She would occasionally break into houses looking for anything from toys to kitchen utensils. Most of the neighborhood was aware of her, including the cops. There was a bank that looked like a house. One night the girl broke into the house that looked bank - but it wasn't a house, it was a bank. The lights flashed, alarms went off, and the cops rushed in to save the empty bank that had every penny in the vault. They stormed the house and found the girl scared to death hiding in the coat closet. A female officer pulled her out of the closet and threw her on the ground. After the lady cop wrestled her to the ground, and while the female officer was on the girls back pulling the girls arms behind her to handcuff them, the male cop pulled his weapon and shot the young lady in the forehead instantly spraying brain matter all over the female cop still sitting on the girls back.

Her mother could not understand why her daughter killed and asked me to take the case and investigate. I agreed to take her case and started the investigation. There had been an epidemic of cops shooting black kids all over the country and this appeared to be another one. In this case, the Lansing police department, the cops that responded to the bank robbery call, we're all aware of the girl physical and mental disabilities. The female cop had several recent encounters with the girl before this shooting.

The cop reported that he shot the girl because the handicapped girl pulled a knife and tried to stab him and his partner. Because he feared for his life and the safety of his partner, he felt authorized to kill her he said. I ordered a gunshot residue test. The test would establish the distance she was from the cop when he shot her. The corresponding test in this case revealed there was no gunshot residue on the young lady's corpse. Normally if someone is within six feet or less of a gunshot there will be residue blasted from the gum on the victim. The residue test indicated that the male cop that shot the handicapped girl had lied about fearing for his life, lied about his fear of being stabbed and lied about the girl endangering his partner's life.

As I was working the mentally handicapped girl's death, I wondered if I could manage it all. I was already weary and tired from the endless hours spent on the first Enbridge case. I just kept pushing on.

I was dead tired when Newton called about assisting and helping me in the second Enbridge case. He was interested. I suggested that he come to Michigan and see for himself. He agreed. I set up a gathering at the Kellogg Convention center. Newton planned to fly into Detroit. I was to pick him up from the airport and then take him back to my place for the night before the big meeting at the Kellogg Center in Battle Creek. Newton always flew Southwest for their cheap fares. He could easily have afforded a hanger full of private jets but flew commercially. I was excited and a little apprehensive to see him. Newton was a billionaire, flying into Detroit and staying at my house. I considered getting some sort of security service, but ultimately did not.

Without security and a week later, I was at the Detroit airport picking up Newton. He looked the same as when I met him with Benton years ago. He was wearing the same 'ole drab brown jacket, slacks, and a half-tied tie. He had a satchel and a small suitcase clutched in his hands. Always in a hurry, he was in a rush to get to my house. On the way we discussed the Panama case. I reminded him I got tossed out of the Tuscarora case and that I lost the multimillion-dollar settlement. I'll never forget his response when he replied saying, "What mattered is that you fought and fought hard and smart. It's nice to win, but the fight is the most important thing to me. And you fought hard for the Tuscarora". He continued, "with O'Quinn, it was always for the money".

We got to my place after circling around my house a few times to make sure the coast was clear. After a quick dinner, he explained more about the Panama case. He told me that many indigenous Ngäbe in northern Panama were exposed to a banned pesticide produced and provided by an American chemical company in Michigan and sold to and used by an American fruit company. Newton believed it was genocide. As with most indigenous anywhere, they were a problem for the government. The government wants to take their land. The Panamanian government and their masters and owners encroached upon their lands. For taking their land, the Ngäbe disrupted transportation and blocked roads and tore up railroad tracks. That gave reason for the Panamanian officials to retaliate. With no sympathy, the Panamanian government clandestinely set out to get rid of them all.

Their clandestine and insidious plan was to attack the indigenous using banned pesticide and thus expose the workers to the genocidal effects of the pesticide. The Ngäbe lived in and on the banana plantations. They were exposed to daily aerial spraying of the poisonous pesticides by planes spraying over where they worked and lived. The result was the men became sterile and pregnant women's fetuses were born defected or still born. After we discussed the Panama cases, we prepared for the meeting scheduled for the next day.

The next day, we both got ready and drove together to the Kellogg Center in Battle Creek. The Kellogg Center was a huge facility that could easily hold twenty thousand people at full capacity. I brought in a large crowd. Over 4000 people from Battle Creek and surrounding area who all were affected by the pipeline oil spill attended the meeting. First some community, county, city, and state officials spoke. They gave simple advice and warned about drinking the water. After they spoke, I spoke and so did Newton. We had the large crowd on their feet clapping and chanting *down with Enbridge*! After the meeting, we drove home. Newton slept on the way back. The next morning, I returned Newton to the airport. I never saw Newton in person again.

On the way back from dropping Newton off at the Detroit airport, I pondered and thought about the Panama case. It would require lots of work. I would be going back and forth to Panama for many years. There were so many problems assisting with the case. But it sure sounded exciting! So, I went for it. I called Newton and told him I was on board and ready to assist. Newton sent all kinds of material. He also had some of his runners and assistants in Panama contact me.

I was unaware that Newton was stealing clients from the discredited law firm. I did not know it, but I was looting his associates' clients. Newton had funded them initially, but that firm had a falling out with the plantation workers. During the accounting of the initial settlement, it became apparent the firm Newton was financing and backing was making unauthorized withdrawals from the settlement funds.

Before the falling out between the lawyers and plantation workers, the original case filed in California Federal Court had to be transferred to Michigan. Once that American fruit company from California settled out and dismissed from the case in California, that left only the Michigan chemical company. Being from Michigan, the chemical company could no longer avail itself to California courts and jurisdiction. The chemical company's business headquarters was in Michigan and that was where the case belonged. That's why Newton asked me if I was still in Michigan and actively practicing in Federal Court.

Even though Michigan had jurisdiction after the first settlement, much of the case was still going to be processed in Panama. I made plans to fly into Panama City, Panama and meet up with Newtons attorneys at the Sheraton when I got there. I was excited, but a bit apprehensive. I was used to smoking weed every day. I was not going to smuggle weed into Panama. There had to be somewhere to find, and purchase weed there in Panama City. The flight from Detroit to Panama took all day. The first leg of the flight from Detroit to Atlanta and then from Atlanta to Panama City,

Panama. Almost to Panama, I looked out my airplane window, I saw miles of ocean that finally gave way to the Panamanian coastline. From thirty-five thousand feet I could see a lush green coastline abutted by a beautiful blue ocean. It looked so inviting and held expectations of excitement.

With high expectations of excitement, I was flying into an airport in Panama with a dubious past. Operation *Just Cause*, President Bush called it, was the US military invasion of Panama to oust the US backed dictator Manuel Noriega in 1989. The cold war was shadowing central America, and the big prize was the Panama Canal which was soon to be given control and operation to Panama in 2000. Whoever controlled the Panamanian government, controlled the vital canal. US intelligence put Noriega in as their puppet in their fight against communism. Noriega fell out of graces with the Bush administration for allowing cocaine cartels to use Panama as a warehouse and staging area for the US cocaine market. Several attempts were made to overthrow him. The US invaded, eventually, with its point of attack at the Panama airport. The same airport that I would soon arrive.

The airport is right on the coast. As the plane came in for our landing, it felt like we were going to land on the ocean water. The plane touched down smoothly. As soon as it touched down, the heat and tropical smells from outside invaded the plane. After a short taxi, the plane pulled into the airport, and we disembarked. As I disembarked, the heat and humidity were more intense with sweet smells abounding. I walked into the airport and went through customs which was a joke. I just waived at the customs officers, and they cleared me into Panama. Within the airport it was a three-ring circus of automobile, electronic, phone and perfume sales displays. Each with beautiful women, enticing me to inspect of them and their products.

After making through customs and baggage claim, I took a taxi to the Sheraton in Panama City. It took about thirty minutes to get there. Sheraton was on the outside of the city. It was one of the safest places for foreigners to stay because it was guarded and monitored by the US government. Getting out of the taxi, I felt the humidity hit hard again. I walked into the hotel and waited for a few minutes and then was summoned up to the desk. They initially started the conversation speaking in Spanish and I indicated my Spanish was not very good, so he started over again in English. I registered and went to my room. After going to the room, I went to explore downstairs. There was an outdoor pool and several indoor restaurants. I ate dinner in the hotel restaurant that evening. The food was foreign to me. I noticed a big difference between the food I was used to eating in the US and the food available there in Panama.

After trying to eat Panamanian food, I went up to my hotel room. I really felt the need to get high. I knew that I could find cannabis at a whore house. I wasn't interested in a sexual encounter - I wanted to find weed. I had been to many whore houses, including the Mustang Ranch in Nevada. I had been visiting boy's towns since I was sixteen. The last thing I wanted was to get sexually involved in Panama with a whore.

I got dressed, put on my suit, and I took off. I flagged down a taxi and asked about girls. He got a strange giggly look on his face and said he knew where to go. He could speak English fairly well. I was lucky, Panama has the largest expat population of any foreign nation. Panama uses the American dollar as its currency and about one third of the population speaks English. The cost of living is low, and labor is cheap. You can easily get a dual citizenship between the US and Panama. It would be a nice place to retire. When I was there, the US and China were vying for control of Panama and the canal.

Out on my hunt for weed, my taxi pulled into a luxurious driveway in front of what looked like a small Taj Mahal. My taxi door was opened by a man wearing a tuxedo and pleasantly pointed in the direction of the front door. It was a castle-like structure and on the first floor was the entryway into a large room filled with blinking disco lights, chairs, and dance floors. I was escorted to a small couch in front of the dance floor. In about a minute a beautiful young woman popped up to my right out of nowhere. She was about twenty-five and looked a lot like Angelina Jolie. Her name was Alejandra. She was about five foot one with dark black hair, fat lips, swerving hips. She asked me what I was doing there in Panama City, starting our conversation. I had flown in from the US and was working on a case I told her. I was going to Changuinola. She asked what kind of case, and I told her about the indigenous Ngäbe chemical exposures.

Her spoken English was broken, yet she seemed to understand what I said very well. She understood that I was there to help the indigenous. Unknown to me, the plight of the indigenous was a hot topic in Panama. Most Panamanians were very sympathetic to the indigenous and it was a very big deal for most Panamanians. They respected the indigenous and were against the government's attempts to take their land away. Out of nowhere she said, "I'll go with you!" Astonished and curious, I listened further. "I help you! You do not make it alone. Dangerous!" She said I could buy her for five days for twenty-five hundred dollars. I agreed and went around to several ATMs to pull out the twenty-five hundred to pay her pimp.

After gathering all the money and paying off her pimp, I took her with me back to the hotel. We talked about the case and about her situation. She was from Medellin Colombia. She flew back and for the for her job every week. She shared a small apartment with another whore. Prostitution in Colombia and Panama was a respected career. With pride, Alejandra flew back weekly to Medellin to see her daughter and family. Her daughter, Isabella, stayed with her parents when she was gone. All of her money, thoughts and attention focused on her little girl and family. Her intense loyalty to her family was admirable. They were very connected to each other by communicating daily.

We stayed up late talking. The next day we went out and rented a vehicle. I rented a Toyota Four Runner. We took the Four Runner back to the hotel and we packed up all our stuff. We hit the road in the morning. It was exciting - we were on the Pan Am Highway. It goes from Canada all the way down through Central America. Getting out of Panama City was difficult, but Alejandra directed me, and we made it out of town. We ventured out of Panama City and up north on the Pan Am towards Costa Rica.

We were traveling to a town called Changuinola, just miles south of Costa Rica and across the mountain range near Boca Del Toro. My destination was about two hundred kilometers up the Pan Am. Before we left, she was able to score some weed. The weed calmed me down substantially and I really enjoyed the drive getting high. The weed gave me an appetite too. I had not eaten much to that point.

It was great having some weed for the drive. I'd never driven on anything like the Pan Am, not even in my excursions to Mexico. It was a narrow, two-lane, no-shoulder highway with pedestrians and all kinds of other businesses and shops just off the road. Kids would run out and try to slap the car as I drove by. I saw many women were dressed in beautiful colored clothes and dresses.

Beside pedestrians, there were other hazards on the highway like mini banana trucks that looked the size of a match box toy. Full of bananas and going about five miles an hour while I was going sixty miles an hour and on the hilly roads, it was easy to come up on one very quickly. It was always important, Alejandra said, to watch your speed because dealing with the local cops never turned out well. As we drove about forty miles outside of town, we came upon a checkpoint. Panama is filled with check points all along the Pan AM in each jurisdiction.

Each Panamanian jurisdiction had their own police force, boundaries, and borders. As we entered a different territory, I was signaled over to be searched and interrogated. Most of the border guards were teenagers in camouflage uniforms holding AK47s. Upon seeing me they asked in Spanish, "where are you going gringo". I could see anger in their faces, and they looked as if he was going to rob me. To my rescue, Alejandra jumped out of the Four Runner and explain in Spanish what we were doing and where I was going. Once the young guards realized I was there to help the indigenous, their face lightened up and their mood and statements were enthusiastic. They said in Spanish, "you go help the Indians. Good man, good man!" If it wasn't for Alejandra, I would have never made it out of the city nor through the different borders with the teenage border guards. We drove all day and went through four more checkpoint stations, and we finally arrived.

We drove over a mountain range to get to Changuinola and arrived late at night. Changuinola was a strange indigenous town. It was mostly occupied by the indigenous Ngäbe tribe. They were there before the conquistadors arrived long ago. We pulled into our hotel and checked in to separate rooms. The next day I would be meeting with the union leaders and a few of the regular members. I got up early, tried to eat, and had a chance to walk around. What wonderful smells and views. Everything was lush, warm, and humid. Flowers bloomed from everywhere, palm trees were over me swaying in the wind, and I had a sense of adventure.

I was ready for the adventurous meeting with the union leaders. But I didn't quite know what to do about Alejandra. I thought they would surely know what she was. I asked her to stay out of the way. Staying out of the way for Alejandra was dressing in her bikini and hanging out at the swimming pool. While she was at the pool, I met with the union members and leaders. The main union leader was an older lady named Maria. She wore a brightly colored indigenous dress, and she had beads around her wrist and ankles. Being the union leader, she made a lot of the decisions on her own. All the other union leaders and members bowed to her authority – like she was an Aztek goddess.

Maria and I discussed the case, her union members injuries, and my retention. She knew of Newton and the other attorneys that he was working with him in Panama. They were supposed to be there too. She told me that the she was supposed to meet up with the other attorneys several weeks ago. They never showed up because they were murdered. She told me the official story was that prostitutes stabbed both of them to death in a robbery. However, she believed that the bad guys hired by the law firm that was being replaced murdered the two attorneys and blamed prostitutes. That other law firm still had a lot of control over those disgruntled indigenous clients by fear, intimidation, and threat.

I was alarmed about the murdered attorneys. The two dead guys were the attorneys I had been talking to and made plans to meet. I was supposed to have met them at the Sheraton when I arrived. I never heard from them. We had all agreed to drive to Changuinola together. They were supposed be at the meeting. They set it up, not me. I had no more contact with them around two weeks ago just about the time that they were murdered. These were Newton's helpers. He should have known about their murders, but he did not tell me. I got a sinking feeling realizing that Newton was playing both sides. He was backing the attorneys who were kicked out of the cases and had me stealing clients from them as well. I was stunned. I was nothing more than a pawn in his double cross games. Benton had warned me years ago that someday Newton would screw me.

Alejandra got a lot of attention sitting out at the pool by some of the union members. Little did they know that she was my companion for the trip. After meeting with the union leaders, I was asked to meet with a bunch of the union members in David (Da-Veed). David is back over the mountain range and in a much warmer location in Panama. Alejandra and I packed up the next morning and took off for David. Arriving, David looked nothing like Changuinola. David was a modern city with shops, stores, and highways. It was a regular modern city – it even had a Mc Donalds. We checked into our hotel rooms. I had a planned meeting with the union folks that afternoon. The union hall was some thirty miles outside of town in the jungle. Alejandro and I drove out to the union hall.

When Alejandra and I arrived at the union hall outside of David, there were over a thousand union members and many of the women carrying with them their children. After introduced by Maria, I got up and gave a speech in English that very few of union members understood. When I took a break, Alejandra then got up and acted as my interpreter. No matter how long I spoke or what I said, she would repeat every word in Spanish that I just said in English. She even mimicked my exact body movements made during my speech. It was so funny and spectacular. It was so hot as hell there at the union hall. Alejandra noticed me sweating, came over to me, and patted my forehead with a dry towel occasionally. At that moment, after my speech, it hit me like a rock - I had fallen in love with a whore!

At the end of my and Alejandra's speech, every mother lined up to show me and Alejandra their children with each child displaying an unnatural birth defect. I had never seen such horrific body manipulations as I saw on those children and babies as I did that day. There were arms growing out of backs, fully disfigured heads, and some three eyed kids. Alejandra began to cry from what she witnessed, excused herself and went back to the Four Runner. We did not say anything to each other the rest of the night. I've never been able to get over the shock of seeing all those chemically mutilated children.

What I had just observed affected me more than the children's deformities I saw at the Tuscarora Nation. Both were hideous, but the sheer number of the deformed children at this that union hall was overwhelming. I've seen nothing worse than the malformed and humiliated bodies of the Ngäbe children. We traveled back to Panama City the next day. I returned Alejandra to her apartment building. We waved goodbye. My flight out was that afternoon. I spent all that time with Alejandra without any sexual contact. I fell in love with her, and I was afraid to leave her and that I might never see her again.

I was missing Alejandra but had a lot to do upon my return. I was preparing to file the second lawsuit on the Enbridge case. I had a lot of new Enbridge clients to process. Most of the new clients suffered the same minor exposure injuries that included runny noses, sore throats, headaches, and nausea. None of them had money for doctors for serious ailments, much less the resources to go to the doctor and have their symptoms recorded.

Without much evidence to support my clients' injuries, I filed a second lawsuit against Enbridge. I was still trying to do a trial a month. That month was another criminal sexual conduct case. A Hispanic male had developed a relationship with a six-year-old boy. After lots of grooming, he started the sexual assaults. The assaults continued and were eventually discovered by the boy's father. Charges were brought and he was arrested. I was appointed as his attorney. My client spoke only Spanish. I petitioned for and the court appointed a translator.

I prepared for the trial and used the interpreter. Her abilities were great; However, she was very opinionated. She was a headstrong Mexican lady. My client was facing a lifetime in prison if he went to trial and found guilty. The prosecutor offered my client a plea deal with a cap of no more than five years in prison. After reviewing the evidence, possible testimony, and everything else, it was my strong opinion that the prosecutor's offer was a gift, and he should accept the plea offer. Rarely would I ever have recommended taking a plea. With my developed trial skills, I could either force a very good deal or have a good chance of winning a trial. In this case, he got a great plea offer.

After much explanation about the great plea offer, my client still did not want to plead guilty and refused to take the plea deal offered to him. He could not understand why it was illegal to have a sexual relationship with a six-year-old boy. He just couldn't understand. I had seen that phenomena before in CSC cases where the adult thinks he can have, and that it is OK to have a regular sexual relationship with a child.

I pushed and pushed strongly for him to take the plea deal. However, the interpreter thought I was trying to strong arm and manipulate his decision. She complained to the judge. The next day, the judge called me up to the bench and reprimanded me for my actions. After being reprimanded, the case went before the jury. They heard all the evidence, however awkwardly presented with the translator. The defendant took the stand and the prosecutor cut him to ribbons. The jury deliberated for less than an hour and came back with a guilty verdict. At the sentencing hearing a few months later, he got life without the possibility of parole.

I was trying to catch my breath and take a break when I got a call from Newton. I had not spoken to Newton since I was in Panama and found out about the murders of his other two attorneys. I did not really trust him anymore, but he had information about the Enbridge cases. I decided to talk to him and see what he had to say. It was about the cause of the pipeline spill and release. It was not good news about the cause of the oil spill. Newton's investigators and contacts in Israel reported to him that the Enbridge oil spill could very well be the result of a computer virus named STUXNET.

Newton explained further that in the middle of Obama's first term as President, Operation Olympic Games was continuing as the first formal offensive act of pure cyber sabotage by the United States against any other country. The argument that it would prevent an all-out war must have sounded reasonable to the Obama administration. During the Bush administration, Iran's nuclear capabilities were nearing militarization. That is what Obama had to walking to entering the White House in January 2009. The militarized material threatened was a direct threat to Israel because of Iran's devote promise to annihilate all Israel and Jews.

In 2009 ,the Iran–Israel relationship had deteriorated to the point that it would be advantageous for Israel to preemptively attack Iran's nuclear research facilities before Iran acquired a nuclear weapon. Normally, that would require air raids and bombings and maybe a military invasion which would cause loss of life and a lot of property damage. The action might also ignite a middle eastern war. There had to be an alternative to an all-out war without bombing or invasion. By the time Obama was in office, Iran was producing weapons grade plutonium. Israel's options were decreasing daily. The Israelis would soon be threatened by Iranian nuclear weapons. There seemed to be no options for Israel but to conduct a preemptive military attack. The United States and Israel devised an alternative to an all-out war. The solution was a cyber-attack, an alternative option to a direct physical confrontation.

The United States Strategic Command along with other intelligence officials came up with a solution. They created a sophisticated virus that would act as an offensive cyber weapon. The goal was to gain access to the Iranian industrial computer controls where the plutonium centrifuges were located. The computer code or virus was designed to invade the specialized computers that command the plutonium centrifuges.

The United States and the Israel government collaborated in its creation and militaristic use. The virus they created was initially called *the bug*. Once publicly discovered, it was called STUXNET. It specifically targeted supervisory control and data acquisition systems, which are used to control machinery and industrial processes. STUXNET was specifically written to take over certain programmable industrial control systems and cause the equipment run by those systems to malfunction, all the while feeding false data to the systems monitors indicating the equipment to be running as intended. No one planned that the virus would escape from the Iranian closed systems.

The *Bug* aka STUXNET cyber-attack was only partially

successful but gave the Iranians more resolve and hatred. A programming error in STUXNET caused it to spread to computers outside of Iran. One of the Iranian engineers with the virus on his computer inadvertently let the genie out of the bottle when he took his work computer home without authorization. He plugged his infected computer into his private internet at home. Yet, as easily as it escaped none of the geniuses at the US or Israeli intelligence offices could predicted that STUXNET, the most destructive militarized computer virus ever, might escape and disseminate so easily.

The STUXNET virus accidentally spread beyond its intended target in Iran due to a programming error introduced in an update by Israel. The error led to STUXNET spreading from the engineer's computer that had been connected to the Iranian centrifuges and then spread to the rest of the world when he connected his work computer to the internet. The virus replicated itself once released on the internet. After it escaped, STUXNET, or a variation of it, has been traded on the black market.

It was estimated that STUXNET required the largest and costliest development effort in malware history. Experts studying Stuxnet believe the complexity of the code indicated that only a nation-state would have the ability to produce it. STUXNET attacked Windows systems using an unprecedented four zero-day program vulnerabilities.

The United States was just as vulnerable to a cyber-attack by STUXNET as Iran. STUXNET compromised transportation networks, water supplies, and power grids all over the United States, but the attacks were never disclosed officially. Cheron, in 2011 was one of the few that admitted to a STUXNET attack. So then must have thousands of other systems worldwide been attacked and compromised. No one was taking credit for the cyber-attacks because it was a superior fuck up by the United States and Israel.

Newton also said there was a high probability that the BP rig explosion and oil spill in the Gulf that occurred a few months earlier was also caused by the STUXNET virus. The *Deepwater Horizon* or the BP oil spill was an environmental disaster which began on

April 20, 2010, off the Gulf of Mexico and considered the largest marine oil spill in the history of the petroleum. The aftermath of the blowout and explosion on the Deepwater Horizon oil rig has been regarded as one of the largest environmental disasters in world history. Due to the months-long continuing none-stop spill, it caused major and extensive damage to sea and wildlife areas and fishing.

It was clear from Newton that the Enbridge oil spill and the BP explosion were probably both the result of the STUXNET virus. Newton did not know if it was a blow back from Iran, a direct attack by a third party, or an accidental attack from the original virus. But in either event, the BP and Enbridge oil spills were both monumental disasters caused by a virus created by the United States and Israel. "I'm not getting involved with this case and you should get the hell out of it as well. There's no way to get any settlement when there's a government cover up going on". He continued, "I ran into same thing when I represented all the veterans in the that Agent Orange case in the 70s. The government will do what it can to hide its mistakes and discredit you. You cannot get in front of this Mike. Cut your losses and run".

Without heeding his advice, I amended my pleadings in the second Enbridge lawsuit to include STUXNET. Instead of suing the Federal Government that had governmental immunity, I sued the manufacturers of the computing systems that allowed and failed to report their vulnerabilities. There was governmental immunity, sure, and I could not sue any government entity actually responsible. Those private entities that assisted were vulnerable and liable and a target for my amended lawsuit, nonetheless.

The judge that presided over the first Enbridge lawsuit and assisted with the settlement suddenly retired. He was replaced by a very conservative judge. Within a week of the judicial replacement, the new judge ordered proof that there was a causal connection between the chemicals released in the Enbridge oil spill and those symptoms suffered by my clients. Such documented evidence of exposure would have required not only my clients to have gone to the doctor and have their symptoms reported and recorded, but also require an expert epidemiologist to make that connection between the released chemicals and their symptoms. I had no such evidence.

None of my clients had medical records substantiating their claims that they were affected by the release. In addition to the unprovable short-term injuries, they also suffered possible long-term injuries. The Enbridge pipeline petroleum was so thick it had to be thinned with benzene. Benzene was a known carcinogen. The fruition and timing of the benzene related cancers takes years. Such exposure should have been monitored. My clients, without any way to prove their cases, were dismissed and the case and clients were gone.

Even though Enbridge was dismissed, I was still working on the Panama case. I had been back to Panama several times and developed a relationship with Alejandra. I wanted to help her emigrate to the US, so we eventually got married in Michigan. After we got married, went looking for an apartment for rent in Panama and located one in a high-rise apartment building right on the coast. The apartment building was right on the beach and twenty-five stories high. It was beautifully furnished and had a whirlpool on the balcony and a pool on top of the building. From the balcony was a vivacious view of the coast and ocean as far as you could see. To the left standing on the thirteenth floor my balcony, I could see about five miles away, the Panama Trump Tower. The Trump Tower was built and shaped looking a huge sale mast. Alejandra was very apprehensive and afraid as we walked into the apartment building. She would tell me why later.

With her apprehensions, we walked up to the entry and were greeted by two Colombians dressed in pimpish suits. They showed us a few of the apartments in the building an. We exchanged information and I filled out an application. Alejandra told them about the Ngäbe exposure case. When we left though, Alejandro looked at me very concerningly and said, "people get murdered in that building. It's owned by Columbians". That evening, I got a call from one of the Colombians I met earlier. They said they had someone that wanted to meet me. A little apprehensive but always ready for an adventure, I agreed.

Agreeing to have them pick me up from the Sheraton, I waited downstairs for my adventure to arrive. The two, still in their pimped-out suits, picked me up in a limousine. We drove on the highway for a while, and eventually exited near the coast. The houses were small when we first turned off the highway. As we continued to drive, however, the houses got bigger and larger until we finally got to a section of the city that held nothing but large estates. We pulled up to a gated fence, we were buzzed in, and the gate opened.

Before me lay a huge mansion right on the beach. It was the home of a local Federal Judge in Panama. I later found out that the Federal Judge's father was a member of the Colombian Cartel and that she had dismissed a criminal case against him for his involvement in two container ships full of cocaine. When we pulled up, the Judge was outside standing in front of an elegant entryway adorned in gold. She wore a beautiful red gown that blew in the wind gracefully. Seeing her, I no longer feared getting roughed up, threatened, or even kidnapped.

Not threatened, I was welcomed. We entered her home. I saw a huge double stairway on my entry. It was a palace. I have never seen such a decadence - not even on TV. We sat down to talk. She was very hip to the plights of the indigenous especially the Ngäbe. Her political party in Panama was against the current dominant party that was responsible for marauding and hassling the indigenous. It was politically advantageous for her to help the indigenous. We talked for a little longer and decided to pass information back and forth. I made a deal with her. We agreed to work together, and she would be local council for me. Like the case Tuscarora case in New York, once I had a local attorney, I could then practice law in that jurisdiction. It was a wonderful opportunity to be able to practice law in a foreign nation.

The first part of our arrangement was that the Judge would provide me an office and a place to stay. She asked if I liked the apartment I was shown earlier. I said very much so. She made available that apartment on the 13th floor that Alejandra and I had just inspected earlier that day.

The Judge also agreed to provide me office space. She assigned me some space wither her in her office. The judge's office was located on the top floor of the F& F Building, locally referred to as

The Screw. It was in the Jewish section of downtown Panama City. The offices were well-guarded by armed men all over. Her entire office was encased in a hidden metal mesh basket. The door to her office was two feet thick and looked like a bank vault door with huge hinges. They told me it was a defense against bombings and armed attacks.

I was on top of the world. I was married to beautiful girl, I had a great free apartment, and an office in on top of the coolest building in Panama City. I could practice law in Panama too. It just like seemed too good to be true, but sometime losers get lucky too! It would not last long. At least I got a brief break from all of the stress. I knew it was not going to last long – and it did not

About a week later, I met the judge, her husband, and her guards at the union hall in David. I expected another huge crowd like the first time I met with them. Not this time – Maria was there and another union leader and that was it. Her face was angry and distressed. Her eyes never met mine as I tried to talk to her. The others with her did not appear happy either and they looked angry and concerned too. There were a few of the union members hanging around quietly watching and listening in the back of the hall. The union leaders had changed their mind. Someone had gotten to them and threatened them. They told us they no longer wanted us involved with the case and they were happy with their old attorneys. I was quite dazed and looked harshly at them. I felt weak in my knees wondering what had just happened.

The judge and I were talking, still wondering what happened and why the union leaders abandoned us, when a few of the union members, the actual banana pickers, approached us. They came over, spoke with us saying that they were not in agreement with the union leaders. They wanted to meet us in another place. The judge, me, and her husband and all her guards drove out into the jungle to a small village. None of the primitive habitats had electricity or running water. Each was a shack with a tin roof over it and a cooking area outside. We met outside one of the shacks with a few of the men and eight of the women. At first, I kept addressing the men. But soon realized all the questions and probably all the decisions were going to be made by the women. I forgot that's the way it was with most indigenous, the women were the decision makers. That's the way it was with the Tuscarora and the Mohawk.

Understanding that the women were in charge, we sat and talked directly to them for a while. The women talked back and forth and then went inside by themselves. The men were never consulted or asked their opinion. The women came back later and said they wanted us to take over their case and to represent them. I drove back to the judge's estate in Panama City. There the judge and I worked that evening on hammering out a retainer contract in Spanish.

Needing an office in Changuinola, the Judge helped me get set up with a house I could use to live in and use as an office meet with clients. It wasn't exactly in the city - it was in the middle of the banana plantation right in with the Ngäbe. Before moving in, I had the electricity turned on, an air conditioner installed, and a refrigerator delivered.

Alejandra and I moved into the free apartment in Panama City. It did not take much since it was already fully furnished with daily groceries, laundry and weed deliveries. You could get anything you wanted delivered to that building any time of day or night. Alejandra liked to do cocaine. She would occasionally have several grams delivered to her at the apartment. Coke was very cheap there in Panama. She bought her grams for around ten dollars each. Her cocaine looked really rocky, no powder and I could smell the ether across the room when she opened a container of it. I had not done coke since my teenage years, and I was not going to start then. I was not ready for another addiction and withdrawal.

After some time at the apartment with Alejandra, I drove back to Changuinola. Through the jungle to my new home and office in David. I pulled into the jungle village. I was the only one with a car and I was the only white man. It wasn't much better than the homes of the Ngäbe in David. At least there was electricity, cool air and running hot water. There were lots of little houses in the area and mine was about a quarter mile in. There was a small school on the left entering the village. Didn't look like any school that you'd see in the US. It was made of cinder block and about a thousand square feet with a corrugated tin roof on top. The kids were delivered to school on a trailer pulled by a tractor through the neighborhood. The kids would run and jump on as the trailer was pulled around. The children all were dressed smartly and in clean pressed uniforms.

After passing by the school, I got to my new jungle house. When I pulled in, I saw a crowd of people dancing around a fire in the neighbor's front yard, right next to my shack. The neighbors were conducting a funeral ceremony. It was their mourning ritual to have a party for several days after the funeral. My bedroom was right next to their house where all the partying was going on. Their funeral parties were actually drunken marathons. I could see stacks of beer bottles all over their yard.

To get away as far as possible from all the drunken noise, I laid out my bed out on the kitchen floor. The first night while sleeping on the floor bed, I was about to fall asleep. I noticed a crack between the door and the floor to the outside. I saw a shadow creeping into the gap. It was a huge spider and must have been as big as my fist. It slipped underneath the door and crawled past me just a few feet away. I was paralyzed, I couldn't move. I was afraid that if startled the huge spider might jump on my head. I watched it slowly walk away into the bedroom. I got up, closed the bedroom door, and put a towel down to block the spider's return. I never opened that door again. It was tough living in Changuinola where the temperatures were exceedingly hot, and food was foreign. I was not used to the food, and I didn't get a hot water heater. All my showers were frozen cold. I began to deteriorate quickly.

I was going weekly back and forth between Detroit and Panama City and then driving to Changuinola. It had been a couple of months since I started staying in the jungle house. One night when I was by myself at the jungle office outside Changuinola, I got a call late at night. It was very ominous and threatening. The caller in a deep Spanish accent called me by name. He said, "we're going to cut your tongue out and stick it up your ass". I could not give a good response, other than *fuck you*, so I hung up. I called Alejandra. She did not answer. I called the judge. She would have a couple of her men, who lived at the apartment building, go check on her.

Normally I wouldn't take such a threat too serious in the US, but I was in Panama, in a small little indigenous village in the middle of the Panamanian jungle far away from anywhere. I grabbed up everything important, immediately ran to my car, and took off. I left most everything else there. I had to get to Panama City. I was afraid they had done something to Alejandra. It took five hours to get back to Panama City. The whole way back I kept trying to reach Alejandra or the Judge. But I did not get into the service area until twenty miles outside of Panama City. Once back in the service area, I still could not reach Alejandra, but I was able to get hold of the judge again. She told me her guys were already there to help search for Alejandra.

    I drove directly to the apartments, parked in front and ran to the elevator. I summoned the elevator and went to the 13th floor. The elevator took forever. I got in and went up to my floor. I walked into my apartment, and Alejandra was not there. About the time I walked in, the judge's men knocked on my apartment door. They had been looking for Alejandra too and could not find her. I finally got a call from Alejandra several hours later. She also received a threatening call. She had taken off and went to her other apartment downtown. I was exhausted, tired, and run down. I flew back dead tired and exhausted to Detroit the next day. I still had another jury trial.

    Back in Lansing, I was preparing for one of the worst torture cases I've ever had. Usually without fear of harm, I could meet with my clients in person – face to face. I had no fear of meeting with Chilly in person. However, there was something in this man's eyes. He looked like he would snap at any moment. Normally I meet my clients in a locked room. The deputies would take their sweet ass time if I was getting assaulted by a crazed and angry client. With this crazed client, I was afraid to meet with him in person. I would only meet with him over the jail phone and view him through a window. I didn't even feel safe behind the window. There was just something about him.

    My crazed client caught his girlfriend smoking crack. She had struggled for a long time trying to quit. But there was no way to quit without assistance and there was none. He couldn't take it anymore, so he tied her up and tortured her savagely for several days. After finally taking a break for cigarettes and beer, my client went to the grocery store. While he was away, his wife was able to break free and run out of the house down a busy road. The police found her blocks away running down the street without clothes and her bindings still around her ankles and hands. A SAEN nurse, a Sexual Assault Examining Nurse, interviewed and photographed her injuries and took her statement within minutes of the cops finding her. The photos at the time taken by the SAEN nurse reflected a mutilated and burned body with obvious signs of severe beating. The pain she must have endured.

Despite all of the evidence, my client wanted to go to trial. He said someone else tortured his wife. Yea right, I thought. He was so threatening at trial, I had him handcuffed for my safety. His handcuffed hands were covered by a coat the entire time so the jury would not see. I was pretty good at that point, and I had a chance if I went along with my client's story. If I could just get one member the jury to believe it must have been some other person that tortured his wife, then I would have a chance at a mistrial. Early into the trial, I leaned over to the inflamed client and said, "if I get you off of this, you owe me a year working for me at my office". It would be nice to have that beast sitting at a desk in front of my office to scare the shit out of anyone threatening me or causing me trouble.

It was going well – for a while. I could see in the jury's eyes that they believed me until the prosecutor called the SAEN nurse as a witness. The SANE nurse testified that she took the statement of the victim just minutes after her escape. She played the twenty-minute recording of the victim over my objections. After playing the tape, the jury members looked at me with disgust. I was a liar, and they were disappointed. They saw I was trying to get a guilty monster off for no other reason but to win the trial.

He was not going to be working at my office anytime soon. It didn't take the jury long and they found him guilty. After their deliberation they sent a note to the judge telling him that they had reached a verdict. None of the jury members looked at me as they walked back into the courtroom. The bailiff took their verdict to the judge. The judge read the verdict, "guilty". I knew before they read the verdict that they would find him guilty. The judge dismissed the jury. Everyone left the courtroom except me. I stayed in the empty courtroom. It was a hallowed feeling. That was my eighty fifth jury trial. I packed up everything into boxes. I had an executive dolly and used it to roll the stack boxes behind me. My mind was swimming. I was feeling nauseous and dizzy, my head hurt as I left the courtroom.

I took the elevator down to the first floor and walked past the security area. Right when I pushed the door open to go outside, my head exploded with pain. My head felt like a bottle rocket that had blasted off up into the sky, and then exploded into many pieces. I fell down. I thought it was a nervous breakdown. I was afraid for anyone to see me.

CHAPTER EIGHT: BACK IN TIME TO THE INNOCENT

I could not take it anymore. I had to escape and get away from everything and everyone. The stress was just too much, and my mind popped. I had to find my safe place. I escaped mentally back to my childhood where it was safe. I was swept back in time. My childhood flashed in front of my eyes. The memories flooded in. I was a kid again, back in Midland, Texas. I was standing on top of the rickety old fort in my backyard - it looked like a mile to the ground. All the new kids were watching. None of the others had dared to jump. Fearless, I jumped….and broke my arm.

Even though I broke my arm, I got a reputation for jumping off. I broke my arm just after moving to a different part of Midland, Texas in 1963 to a new neighborhood. The new house had a huge backyard separated by a low wooden fence. In the back part of the yard was a left-over rickety wooden fort. It had two levels. There was a jump-off plank on the second level. It was quite a feat to climb up and bravely jump off.

The front part of the yard had an enchanted China Berry tree. It had grown around frayed rope resembling long blond hair. I believed a little girl had been caught in the tree with only her hair remaining. My dad called it an enchanted Irish Fairy tree - one that would capture children and take them into the tree world to eat. Dad said I needed someone to play with instead of talking ad playing with trees. Mom dragged me around from house to house looking for a playmate. I didn't want to go. With one hand clinching my hand, she knocked on the door with the other. Joe's mom answered the door. Joe was one year older than me and only a block away. Another boy to play with. He lived close enough to walk.

Joe was the youngest of four kids. He had three older sisters. Terri, Nanett and Cindy. Joe's Dad was unhinged though. We were on guard ready for a tongue lashing or a fake backhand. He always had a six pack of Budweiser with him and a lit cigarette in his mouth. In our neighborhood, all the houses on the same side of the block were connected by backyard fences. Each house shared at least one fence with its neighbor. If you did not live on the end of the block, you shared each side with two neighbors. Most of the fences were made of cinder blocks. The gates to the allies and front yards were made of vertical planks with two-by-fours at top and bottom running horizontally.

We used the fences as our personal path from one house or fort – to another. We walked along the top of the cinder block fences. Hands and arms stretched out to the side like airplane wings for balance. The wooden part of the fences took more skill to walk on the top horizontal wooden planks. We proceeded with one foot slowly in front of the other in a heel-to-toe fashion.

We built a lot of forts in Joe's backyard because it did not have a fence along the alley and was thus open to the ally. In the open part of Joe's back yard, we dug our tunnels and built our forts. We used scrap lumber, carpet, cardboard, and any nails that we could find, steal, or borrow. Trash can hunt gave many treasures to our forts. Prowling all the neighbor's trash cans, we discovered nearly empty liquor and beer bottles which made wonderful fort trophies. We struck gold if we discovered a Playboy or Penthouse. Our forts were well insulated and enclosed with an entry and emergency escape door through an underground escape tunnel. The escape tunnel was connected to more underground passageways.

Besides building forts and passageways, a lot of my time was spent with Pop - my dad's dad. He was born 1903 in Quart Ireland. Over six feet, he was a large broad chested man, and he had a full head of white hair. He always wore khaki pants, farmers ankle high tie up boots and long-sleeved shirts. He topped it with a farmer's light grey felt hat with a black crow feather sticking up the back.

Pop and his family went through Ellis Island in New York to

Comanche County Texas. They paid for their rip from Ireland by working it off for two years in Commanche County. They raised cotton for a large outfit there. Pop's family was provided a one room house with no running water or electricity. It was not slavery like so many Africans were forced into, but forcibly required to them repay. Indenture was debt bondage and unfree labor. Pop's dad and his family were required to work to pay off their debt and pledged the family as collateral. It was a big deal when they paid their debt and became free. Their first place was a dug-out home. He remembered when they got a cast iron stove and food no longer had to be cooked over an open flame outside.

Pop always told stories of Irish magic and he was a tree talker. Pop said he had a spiritual connection with the trees. My dad was embarrassed about Pop's beliefs and most of the town was afraid of him. I did not know why until much later. Pop moved to Fisher County Texas in his twenties. He never talked about that time much. Like something happened to him then. In the 1930s he share-cropped for a few years and saved enough money to buy the home place. He had just started his family when the stock market bottomed out and the Great Depression began.

Pop had three sections of land. Nearly two thirds were in pasture and the remaining acreage was cultivated. He grew cotton, sorghum, sugar cane and alfalfa. On the pasture, he ran cattle. All the pastures were surrounded and intersected by miles of barbed wire. The land was burnt red clay. The south fork of the Brazos River ran through the back of the Pop's home place. It was nothing more than a little creek you could easily jump over unless there was a flood.

When I was younger, I spent a lot of weekends, Christmas, Easter vacations and most of the summer at Pop's place. Joe usually went with me until we got older. He was treated like a brother by everyone. Joe and I roamed Pop's pastures with our BB guns, racoon hats and David Bowie knives. Pop's place was great. He always had cases of Dr. Pepper to greet us in the main entryway. We drank lots of iced tea too. Into huge jars of iced tea, we dumped as much sugar in as we wanted.

While at Pop's we would go to town almost daily and eat

at the Hi-The-Ho restaurant. There was a jukebox inside the air-conditioned indoor seating area. It was a salvation in that hot-as-hell little cattle-cotton town. The fried chicken, crinkled fries, gravy, and Texas toast were regulars for me. The fried chicken dinner was always followed with a fried cherry pie with soft serve vanilla ice cream on top. All the time listening to great music blasting those small-town folks out of their seats. The duke box music lifted me out of the heat and dust. Every day I looked forward to that treat and heat relief.

If Pop had errands in town, he would drop me off. He always gave me money to go spend at the five-and-dime next to the hardware store. They all had wooden floors and smells that came from decades ago. There was also an old movie house in Rotan. Its heyday was back in the twenties. The seats and armrests were wooden without padding. The gargoyles, sitting up in the corners, radiated an ominous impression. There was always a Clint Eastwood spaghetti western playing with double feature horror movie like *The Blob*. Going back to Pop's place after watching spaghetti westerners all day was surreal. The sets of the spaghetti western came to life and looked just like the scenery at Pop's place. Clint Eastwood could jump out with guns blazing at any moment.

Besides the in-town visits, Joe and I were given free rein to do what we wanted at the home place as long as we weren't stupid. Joe and I stayed up many a late summer night fueled by Dr. Pepper playing poker for matches. We bet on five and seven card stud, Mexican sweat and five card draw. We played them all with skill. Along with playing poker all night long, we explored the pastures around the home place. Pop warned us to stay away from the water cistern. It was a deep hole filled with water for the house. It could cave in if we played around it. He also warned us not to molest the Native American burial mounds.

The Pawnee and Comanche were still around when Pop moved onto the land. Pop's home place, out in the far pasture, had an official indigenous ceremonial historical site. Part of the land on his home place was considered sacred by the indigenous and there were still active burial ceremonies being conducted when Pop bought the land. He set aside that land where the burial site was located and granted blanket permission for any indigenous burials. The last Comanche burial was in 1929, right before the stock market collapsed. Pop was given the black crow feather to signify his friendship with the Native Americans. The burial mounds were not dangerous, but there were dangers all around. There were rattlesnakes, scorpions and killer centipedes. We were also warned about feral and javelin hogs. We were told to climb up the nearest tree if we ran into any. Pop said, "those feral pigs get up to 400 pounds and both will eat anything – including you boys". Joe and I thought he was joking. After his warning, we were walking through the pasture towards the creek when we heard pigs squealing and snorting behind us. We climbed the nearest cottonwood tree. Just as we got off the ground, a family of javalina hoggs appeared below us - only a few feet away. I could smell them in the heat and dust. They growled and flashed their teeth at us. They stayed a long time hoping to dislodge us. We shot our BBs at them, only making them mad and irritating them further. We stayed up in that tree long after they left. Finally, hearing Pop honking his pickup truck's horn from far away, our signal to come home, we gathered nerve enough to climb down and run all the way back to Pop's.

I did not spend all my free time at Pop's. I spent some time in Midland during the summers at Alamo swimming pool. It was quarter mile further than my elementary school. But every day for years for only twenty-five cents, we could swim all afternoon. We usually walked up to the pool after lunch and stayed 'till closing at six. Every year, we got so tan with sun bleached hair.

It was exciting at the end of summer anxiously awaiting the new school year approaching. In Midland the elementary schools were named after those at the Alamo. James Bonham, my elementary school's namesake, was killed at the Battle of the Alamo. My junior high school's name was Alamo Jr. High. Both were about one mile from my house. Joe was a year older, so he started school before me. That was a strange year. I would wait for Joe to get home, and he would make new friends. I felt left behind.

It was my turn to start school. I made many friends when I finally got to school. I met Jimmy Baker in first grade. He was always getting into trouble. He was infamous. Jimmy would hide in the bathroom stalls waiting for anyone to walk in. The bathroom was arranged so that to get to the urinals, you would have to walk past a row of toilet stalls. When someone walked by, Jimmy would jump out of a stall and attempt to urinate on your leg. He did this for a few days until Mr. Ladd, the principal visited the boy's room.

Jimmy Baker was busted by Mr. Ladd who looked to be one hundred years old. The janitor gave any licks in his place. Mr. Ladd always had a television in the cafeteria for the world series. He also played the news for us using his own TV from home. It helped keep us up to date with what was going on in the world. I could not wait for summer the summer of '67 after being pinned up in the classroom all day.

The summer of 1967 was the height of the hippie scene. Mom put me in a summer acting class at the parks and recreation. The acting school received requests for tryouts for a part in an upcoming movie being produced out of Hollywood California called *Midnight Cowboy*. It would star Dustin Hoffman and Jon Voit. Part of the movie was to be filmed in Big Spring, Texas. It was about forty-five miles away.

The tryouts were scheduled right in the middle of the afternoon. I threw such a fit for having to miss going to Alamo pool that I got to swim right up and until time to go. At the tryouts, they asked me to pretend I was mad, to act scared, act happy and laugh out loud and last to cry. I was one of three who tried out for the part. No one knew it at the time, but Midnight Cowboy would be rated X. An X rating then was equivalent to an R rated movie today. The movie, however, went on to win several Academy Awards including best picture in 1968 and was the only X rated movie ever to do so.

Before you know it, another year passed by. 1968 was the year Batgirl joined forces with Batman and Robin for their third year on air. I had a pair of Batman slip-on shoes that mom ordered from the Sears catalog. I ruined them not much later at a family reunion chasing tadpoles. It was so rousing watching the Joker and the Penguin torment Gotham City.

1968 was also the year that Martin Luther King Jr. and Robert Kennedy were assassinated. No more stirring sermons of dreams and no more Bobby. All my favorite shows were blocked because of the assassinations - again. We didn't have video recorders back then. Episodes would not repeat as a "re-run" for half a year, if at all. *Blondie* on Rowen and Martin's Laugh-in and *Hoss* on Bonanza, Gomer Pyle, Ironside and Family Affair are just a few of the great shows. Too many other great shows that year, like: *Dragnet, I Dream of Jeannie, The Mod Squad, Green Acres, Red Skelton, Bewitched and Man from U.N.C.L.E.* Watching those TV shows was so exciting and though campy, had a subliminal gravity that echoed the contentious times.

In addition to the turbulent political scene, American air, water, and land pollution was becoming a big and radical topic. Pollution problems were always in the news and in repeated in the popular music. The Ecology movement got some momentum claiming that we were all polluted mentally and environmentally. 1971 was the year of the Crying Indian commercial was aired on Earth Day. *People start pollution; People can stop it.* Marvin Gaye waged his war against pollution with his song *What's Goin On.*

The music reflected the political and ecological dilemmas. Music was a revolutionary. *Hey Jude* by the Beatles was the longest song on the radio. Jimmy Hendrix's *Electric Lady Land*, his third album, was released that year. The Doors, Cream, Donavan, Deep Purple, Iron Butterfly, Steppenwolf, and Jefferson Airplane all were popular radio songs. One of the best songs from then was *Sitting on the Dock on the Bay* by Otis Redding.

Another year passed. 1969 brought Woodstock and *Easy Rider*, with Peter Fonda. I was too young to see Easy Rider during the original release, but I saw it on the marquee at the Hodge Theater in Midland. I had a wall poster of Captain America – Peter Fonda with his red, white, and blue gas tank and helmet. Soon after the movie came out, my cousin got a chopper motorcycle. Craig was called himself a freak and had an Ecology sign painted on the outside of his house in Rotan. He had a bullet roach clip too.

The next summer was 1970 and Pop's place flooded. It was so bad that Pop's old pickup could not make it into town. He asked me to ride the horse into town. I was surprised that he would rely on me for such a necessary adventure. I felt empowered. I was going to ride Midnight into town for groceries. Midnight was a ten-year-old gelding quarter horse. He was basically a big pet that had not been ridden for a few years. I had ridden him only once before two years earlier – and he bucked me off. But Midnight and I were ready for that adventure.

Rotan was the closest town with a grocery store. There were other towns around – Roby was the closest berg to the farm, but it only had a gas station and the county courthouse. Rotan it was. Pop pulled out the saddle from the barn. The saddle must have been 100 years old back then and it was covered with dust and somewhat chewed up. After throwing the saddle over Midnight's back, I tightened all the saddle straps and placed the bridal in his mouth. We were ready to go. I looked like Tom Sawyer wearing blue jean cutoffs, tank top and tennis shoes. Normally flat, dusty, and dry, the road to town and surrounding fields were covered with white caps. Lakes of water surrounded the Pop's farm looked like an island in all that water. It looked so alien.

Even though it looked scary and alien, Midnight and I rode off. Midnight took me across the fields bypassing the flooded road. There were high spots dividing the fields giving us passage. The going was slow. About an hour later we made it into town and to the only grocery store. Most of the town roads were flooded. Riding right up to the store, I tied Midnight to a wooden stand. By the time I got to the store, a small crowd had gathered. Being one of the first to make it into town, they wanted to know what I saw. "Nibb's boy made it in…the city-boy made it from Jim's place" someone said. I told them of the high water and blowing waves over the fields.

After a small hero's welcome, I got the groceries and supplies. They were stored in the leather pouches attached to the saddle over his lower back. The clouds started to part, and the sun rays peaked through. Midnight and I started back through alien water world. Midnight meandered slowly back home. The saddle pouches must have irritated him because he meandered near the barbed wire fence trying to rub me and the saddle bags.

The next summer, Joe went to stay with his grandmother in Wichita Falls. It was the summer between fifth and sixth grade. The norm was to walk up to the swimming pool every day with Joe. I went to the pool by myself. We had become experts at doing cannonballs and can openers to make a big splash of water when jumping in. When doing a cannonball, your arms wrapped around your legs pulling them into your chest. Doing can-openers required throwing your head back when your feet hit the water. I would try to jump into the water close to the side.

One time when Joe was not there, I did not jump out far enough and struck the back of my head against the side of the pool. I woke up on the bottom. My vision was askew and jagged looking from the bottom up at the top of the pool. I struggled to the top. I had drifted underwater a long way from the edge. I struggled to get to the edge. The lifeguard stand was surrounded by girls. He did not see me until a girl screamed when she saw blood.

Something happened when I bumped my head. I became curious, mom said. I started reading and researching up at the public library in Midland. I saw a movie about the Salem witch trials. I became inquisitive about the witches' strange behavior and what caused them to act as if they were possessed. I discovered the answer - ergot. Ergot was a fungus that grew on wheat. Ergot has alkaloids that if ingested, would cause hallucinations. Further researching at the Midland library, I found a modern connection to a compound that caused the irrational behavior of the witches at Salem. It was the active alkaloids in ergot – LSD. The first person to synthesize LSD out the active ergot alkaloid was Albert Hofmann. While working in his lab trying to discover pharmaceutical compounds, he accidentally ingested his product of synthesis. After his first accidental trip, he intentionally ingested a large dose. He had a bad trip at first. People appeared to morph into fantastic creatures, office furniture moved and shifted like living entities, and he felt possessed by otherworldly forces.

The day he intentionally tripped is now widely known as "Bicycle Day", because as Hofmann began to feel LSD's effects, he tried to ride to the safety of his home on his bike. This was the first intentional LSD trip in history. I followed Hoffman's life the best I could with the material available in that library. I further found out that Hofmann continued to take small doses of LSD throughout his life. He described it as a "sacred drug". He continued, "I see the true importance of LSD in the possibility of providing material aid to meditation aimed at the mystical experience of a deeper, comprehensive reality."

Joe and I experimented with our own magic. We would go to the VFW with Joe's Dad and play BINGO. We saved up our own money to play five-dollar bingo cards. Before the drawing began, we each burned a match from a pack of astrological matching symbols. My match pack was Virgo and Joe's was a Pisces. We each burned our astrological match and we each murmured a made-up incantation. It worked - we won over two hundred dollars. Almost everyone was amazed. Joe's dad was not amazed. On the way home, he pulled the car over. He demanded that we give him the money we won. He threatened us further about "that stupid shit with the matches" and to never do it again. I was stunned and afraid of what Joe's dad might do to us. We gave up the money and we never talked about it ever again.

We never practiced our accidental magic again either. Even though I spent more and more time at the library, I still wanted a good adventure. It was the summer of 1971 and right before junior high school seventh grade. I took a boy scout trip to the Rio Grande in Big Bend National Park, Texas. I was the newest member of the troop, joining the troop just one week before the Big Bend National Park excursion. There had been recent heavy rains in New Mexico and Colorado causing flooding in the Rio Grande flood basin days before our trip.

It was a long slow-going trip in an old school bus pulling a trailer of canoes. The radio played tunes of the time and news of the Water Gate break-ins. We arrived at the park long after dark. We set up camp right next to the Rio Grande. After setting up our tents and starting the fires, a few of us jumped in. The powerful current was unfamiliar and startling. I only knew of shallow, slow running creeks like around Pop's place. The Rio Grande swept me away. I felt helpless being pulled away from the shore at night. I was saved by a log stuck in a sandbar. I crawled along the log until I pulled myself out of that wicked current.

The next morning, we got the canoes off the trailer and paddled off. The troop leaders mumbled that there must have been a big rain upriver earlier because it was flowing fast. One of them said we should wait. Another troop leader said that couldn't be that bad as we jumped in and paddled off. We entered the river in a large open area right by our campsite. The empty trailer was driven down river to meet at the finish point. Ten canoes took off, each with two paddlers. I had never been in a canoe before, but I was a good swimmer. We floated through several canyons with large sky-scraping walls.

It was about lunch time when we paddled over to the shore. We cooked hotdogs over a fire. During lunch, a big swirling whirlpool formed near where we went ashore with the canoes. It sucked down a tree trunk with a loud gulp. The lead trooper's eyes grew big. We paddled wildly to escape swirling water. We noticed the river level got higher and picked up speed. When re-entering the canyons, a faint at first – rumbling arose. The rumbles got louder until thunder. We entered the white-water rapids like going over the top of a roller coaster zenith. Big boulders splashed by on both sides with mountain high canyon walls on each side as we were sprayed and tossed. Being flung down the river in a herky-jerky up and down motion, the water sprayed in my face. We all fought to keep our canoes upright. It was beyond our abilities. We all were thrown out of the canoes into the raging waters. I was swept down the river - bobbing up and down being thrown between the large boulders.

After being washed and tumbled for several miles through the canyons, the river threw us out. I was washed into a marshy area on the United States side. Still out of control, it pushed me towards the flooded banks where the water was flopping and boiling – it was a bunch of water moccasins. I panicked. I screamed. I blacked out. Someone pulled me out of the swirling water. Some of the boys were tossed onto the Mexican side of the river. All the next day troop leaders were in Mexico retrieving those thrown out on the Mexican side.

I was still in a daze all the slow bus ride home back to Midland. America's *Horse with No Name* was popular and playing on the bus radio. *Horse with No Name* carries memories of the long road trip home, the enchantment of Big Bend Park and the Rio Grande River that tried to drown me.

CHAPTER NINE: ALMOST LOST IT ALL

After my head exploded and after reliving my childhood, I was out of it for several months. Ashamed and thinking I had a nervous breakdown; I never went to the hospital or doctor. I could not read or hardly walk. As my cognitive abilities slowly returned, I found myself living on the Rock Pile. The Rock Pile was near Snyder, Texas. It was a piece of property that Pop gave me. It was my safe place. Everything was upside down after my breakdown-stroke.

Back in Michigan, I left every case unattended. I had too many cases spinning like plates on the end of a stick and they all fell to the floor and crashed. I had a lot of people depending on me as their attorney. I let them all down. Soon, I was overwhelmed with grievances and lawsuits. Alejandra held on as long as she could. I became withdrawn and I was not very fun to be around. She eventually she moved back to Medellin, Columbia to be with her daughter.

I had about reached the end of everything including my savings. I sold the property Pop left me to pay off clients whose cases I screwed up. Even after paying back everyone, I was disbarred from the Michigan and Texas Bars. I could not practice law anymore. I was no longer an attorney.

There was some money left after paying back all the disgruntled clients. With the left-over funds, I bought a house in Midland, Texas. It was a nice town home right across the street from a park. It had a whirlpool tub in the atrium outside. It felt empty though because I was missing my daughters and grandson. Back in Michigan, my youngest daughter got into opiates. When she was a classical dancer, she broke her back. She was prescribed opiates for the pain.

Those prescription opiates became addictive. She went to illicit means of satisfying her addiction. I found out through her mother that she had an overdose. Ther is an internal alarm that goes off loudly when one of your children is in trouble and mine was ringing loudly. I could not stand for it. She was my daughter, and I would do anything to help save her life. I arranged to have her stay with me in Texas so she could withdraw.

It was either a rehab center or my place. She flew down with her mother from Lansing. She stayed with me for two months. It was terrifying to see her go through withdrawals. None of my withdrawals were ever as bad. She started cold turkey and her withdraws were so bad that nothing, not even weed, could help her. I ended up taking her to an addiction specialist. He prescribed Suboxone and a lot of counseling. Suboxone was the new methadone. Everything was very expensive, but it helped her a lot.

I watched her suffer every day through her withdrawals. Crying, getting mad, vomiting all of the time and always in pain. After two months of torture, she was doing better and wanted to go back to her son in Michigan. He was staying with his father back in Kalamazoo. She lost custody to the father because of her addictions; the one who was so cruel to her and my grandson. My daughter was going back to the toxic relationship just to be with her son. I knew it was too soon for her to go back. She was not through fighting and conquering the opiate addiction yet. Nonetheless, she wanted to go back. I took her to the airport. It was so sad to see her leave knowing where she was going and what she would have to put up with just to be with her son. I knew she would fall right back into the same addictive pattern.

After she left, I did not hear anything for two months, not a word. I could not get back to Michigan soon enough. I sold my house and took a U-Haul with my three dogs to Michigan. I rented a place near her in Kalamazoo, Michigan. She did not like me being around at first. It caused problems with her boyfriend, the father of my grandson. That was the way it went for a while. I was not welcome in her life. That was about to change.

One evening I got a call about my daughter being rushed to

the hospital. I later found out her appendix had burst because her boyfriend would not let her go to the hospital. He did not believe her complaints about the pain, so he would not let her leave. Eventually my daughter's screams were so loud, the neighbors called the police. An ambulance came to the rescue, and she was rushed to the hospital. Her appendix had burst, and all the poison was seeping into her body.

It was Christmas Eve when I went to see her in the hospital. She was emaciated. When I gave her a hug in her hospital bed, she felt hollow and empty. She was in so much pain. It was so hard to see her like that. She nearly died. She was in the hospital for several weeks. After her release, her and my grandson came to live with me. She was bedridden for months. I took her almost every meal in bed. I received regular death threats from her boyfriend. He threatened to kill me, my daughter, my grandson, and my dogs too. I would do anything to keep her and my grandson safe.

Financially, it was difficult. I was quickly going through the money left over from the sale of the Rock Pile. I could not practice law anymore because I was disbarred, but I could associate and work with other attorneys. I started a business to assist attorneys with their practice. I could do paralegal work, like typing, copying, and writing briefs. I eventually ended up setting up a law office with an attorney I had known from when I was a lawyer and practiced in Lansing. He had an opiate addiction himself. He couldn't manage himself or a law practice. I talked him into starting a law practice. He would be the attorney and I would do everything else. There were a few clients and we obtained retainers from them. The retainers were placed into a trust account for attorneys. After a while the attorney could not manage to even go to court. He could no longer make any court appearances.

Covid hit. Everything stopped. The attorney was in and out of the veteran's psych ward and most of the time he could not even get out of bed. Everything I invested in him, the law firm and office, was lost. I was supporting my grandson and daughter, and it looked like I would be penniless soon. I was fully supporting my daughter and grandson. They lived with me. I paid for everything. I paid for all her opiate withdrawal doctor visits, medications, and therapy too.

I ran out of money. I was not going to let her go but I could not support her and my grandson anymore. My daughter moved to Coldwater, Michigan from Kalamazoo chasing some guy. I borrowed a little money, I packed up along with the three dogs, and I moved to Coldwater too. She stayed in Coldwater for about a year with that guy and my grandson lived with me. Her relationship fell apart and then she moved to Lansing where her mother could help her out. I had no money left and I could not move to Lansing to watch over her. This was a low spot in my life. I was trapped in Coldwater living on my meager social security. I did not have a car. Me and my dogs struggled to live. I had given up on life and it only got worse. I got a call from my daughter's mom in Lansing - my daughter was dead. My grandson found her dead on the floor of their apartment. A small amount of white foam had oozed out of her nose. The autopsy indicated she died of a fentanyl overdose.

She had ingested meth laced with fentanyl and it killed her. It was the most horrible time of my life, and the grief carries on still. I was devastated and couldn't believe my daughter was dead – my little girl. It was all very surreal and sad. Going through the whole funeral process was terrible. Picking out the casket, what dress she was going to be buried in, hair, and flowers. I cry every day thinking of her. Laying in her pink casket, surrounded by flowers, and floating in my tears. I have never been and hope to never be that distraught again. I could not eat. My baby girl was dead. No Native American magic, no weed and no LSD could bring her back – I saw her death years ago though. I knew.

I got a call from Jimmy Baker. He heard about my daughter and gave his condolences for my daughter's death. I had not heard from Jimmy in years. He told me that his daughter had also died. We were both in a bad place full of grief.

I have come to accept my daughter's death even though I still think about her and cry about it every day. But I am content. I have come full circle. Weed is now safe and readily available in many forms. I have my three dogs, and I know when I die, I will have no regrets. I am ready to move on. I want to spend the rest of my life with my dogs, helping my grandson and finishing my second book – and growing and smoking a lot of cannabis.

AFTERWORD

To learn more about events outlined in this book:

Haywood, T. (2014, Aug). Summer of Terror, 10 Years Later. https://www.lansingcitypulse.com/stories/summer-of-terror-10-years-later,1776?

Used with Permission

Made in the USA
Columbia, SC
25 April 2024

0a83c753-c98d-466a-89c7-e38aece50cbcR01